G*S.T.Y.L.E.

developing a passion for God's fashion

G*S.T.Y.L.E.

developing a passion for God's fashion

written by Lisa Hampton-Qualls | illustrated by Anita Hampton

Tate Publishing & Enterprises

Dedication

This book is dedicated to all who desire to wear Gods fashions with a passion that only He can provide.

Published by Tate Publishing & Enterprises, LLC
127 E. Trade Center Terrace | Mustang, Oklahoma 73064 USA
1.888.361.9473 | www.tatepublishing.com

Tate Publishing is committed to excellence in the publishing industry. The company reflects the philosophy established by the founders, based on Psalm 68:11,
"The Lord gave the word and great was the company of those who published it."

Book design copyright © 2008 by Tate Publishing, LLC. All rights reserved.
Cover design by Lynly Taylor
Interior design by Kandi Evans

Published in the United States of America
ISBN: 978-1-60462-267-6
1.Christian Living: Practical Life: P
2.Christian Living: Spiritual Growth:
08.02.06

Acknowledgements

First, I give honor and glory to God for inspiring me to be obedient and write what has been put on my heart, mind and spirit to share with others. I never thought I could sit still long enough and stay focused to write but God set my mind and kept it set for me to finish. I've learned I truly can do all things through Christ who strengthens me!

To my husband, Phillip, my soul mate, much love and many thanks for standing by and encouraging me daily through the months with a willing heart, listening ear and wise counsel. I love you as much as the sky!

To my three sons, Jason, Andre' and Travis, my precious gifts from God; I thank you for the many hugs and kisses, for lifting me up in prayer and encouraging me to keep going even when I felt like quitting. Mom loves you!

Mom, I thank you for supporting, praying and listening to me. Thank you for keeping up with me in the fast lane during those times God gave me such understanding and revelation that words came out of my mouth at 85mph! It's not very often a mom tells her daughter that she inspires her to continually seek God and that makes me feel so blessed. I love you, Mom!

To my dad, daddy's little girl has grown up and grown into wearing her own fashions for God because you've been modeling them for me all my life. I love you for loving me enough to plant God in my heart at an early age and for being there to watch Him grow in me!

To my mother-in-law, Mom Q, there are no words to describe how you've touched my heart. Your beautiful words, listening ear, sweet embraces and kind words have comforted me and blessed me so much over the years and I wholeheartedly thank you.

Last and certainly not least, to my sister, Anita, who has walked with me through every page of this awesome journey and accessorized this book with her special touch. I thank you for loving and supporting me, for sharing your excitement and passion with me. From Lee Sue to Nina Bug, I love you!

Contents

Preface

I have learned so much about who I am in Christ through study and prayer in the Word, and I'm so excited to share what I've learned. As you read this book, I pray God will give you the eyes to clearly see the Truth in Him.

I wear contacts now, but have worn glasses since I was fourteen years old. Wearing them helps me see with 20/20 vision, something I couldn't do without them. Walking with God and studying his Word has given me clearer vision in life. When I didn't take the time to enhance my relationship with him, I saw through eyes without glasses. Now that He's given me the vision to see the things he's placed in my path, I walk confidently through the life he's planned for me. "I don't yet see things clearly. I'm squinting in a fog, peering through a mist. But it won't be long before the weather clears and the sun shines bright! I'll see it all then, see it all clearly as God sees me, knowing him directly just as he knows me!" (1 Corinthians 13:12–13).

Seeing with clearer vision, I was inspired to write this book. It happened while I was in the middle of writing my SpaDayR3 book. Those of us creative, ADD (Attention Deficit Disorder) minded souls have learned to *go with the flow* when God lays inspiration on our hearts, even when we're in the middle of doing ten other things! He commands us to go and tell the

Good News, and he sometimes uses ordinary people like me to do just that.

I chose to write about fashion primarily in obedience to the Father, but also because I love clothes and shopping, and find so many analogies in fashion relating to our walk with God. He *fashioned* Eve from the very beginning, and he uniquely fashioned us as well. Jesus used parables to relate his messages to help people understand biblical truths. While I don't claim to speak in parables, God has lain on my heart and mind some biblical truths and life application using fashion.

I am very passionate about God's fashion because His are the very best and everlasting. My hope is you'll find this book helpful in developing your passion. I pray you'll be able to *see it all clearly as God sees you* the plan laid out for your life, and acquire an abundance of fashionable looks designed to fit whatever shape or size you're in to wear everyday and everywhere. On the occasion someone comments on your stylish outlook, take the opportunity to share your passion for God's fashion.

Fashionably Yours,
Lisa HQ

Fashion in Review

I see *fashion* as part of my daily intake of essentials vitamins. Vitamin A is the adorable sweater I got on sale. Vitamin D is the divine dress that called my name and begged me to buy it. B12 is the number of shoes I bought at a bargain price and Vitamin K is my kickin' black leather boots! Then there's Fiber to keep me regular in shopping at the mall and Lutein to keep a sharp eye on the latest fashions!

While you may not see fashion as essential vitamins, a daily intake of God's word is essential. "All scripture is God-breathed and is useful for teaching, rebuking, correcting and training in righteousness, so that the man of God may be thoroughly equipped for every good work" (2 Timothy 3:16–17).

Developing a passion for God's fashion is a strong desire to live a holy life fashioned in God's grace, styled with his mercy and clothed in his favor. By including him in my daily fashion choices, I've developed a passion for His fashion.

Fashion is also a manner of dress. God's manner of dressing the body of a believer is fully fashioned from the top down. See if you can find the manner in this body:

First there's the head, which is God the *F*ather, and the neck *A*dorned in righteousness; the shoulders of the *S*on upon which salvation rests; the hands to wrap the belt of truth around the waist, which the *H*oly Spirit buckles on us; and the hips that carry divine *I*nspiration to do what is good and right. The thighs evenly proportioned to move in *O*neness with God, and the feet that walk in *N*ewness of life and carry the gospel of peace to others.

In the body of a believer is where we see God's fashioning style, "For in Christ there is all of God in a human body; so you have everything when you have Christ, and you are filled with God through your union with Christ" (Colossians 2:10, TLB)

One thing I've discovered in my daily intake is in God's fashion big "buts" are not allowed! You might say "Big But—So What," but big buts limit our fashion choices. They're not filled with passion rather they're seated in doubt. Big buts doubt God's ability to accomplish his will through us. When it comes to belief in God, there's no room in our faith-filled wardrobe for doubt. You've probably seen or worn some variation of these big buts found in Exodus:

"But I'm not the person for a job like that!"

(Exodus 3:11, TLB)

"But Moses pleaded, 'O Lord, I'm just not a good speaker. I never have been.'"

(Exodus 4:10, TLB)

"But Moses said, 'Lord, please! Send someone else.'"

(Exodus 4:13)

Anytime we're asked to do God's work, he'll fashion us with more than we'll ever need; "I will certainly be with you" (Exodus 3:12, TLB), "…for I will help you speak well and I will tell you what to say"

(Exodus 4:11, TLB).

When we understand all things are possible through God, we'll work hard at eliminating the big buts from our life!

In my younger years I was obsessed with shopping. I guess you could've classified me as a shop-a-holic. While I didn't understand what was driving me, the more I shopped, the more I was spurred to want more. As I've matured in my faith (and my good sense), I found the same force that drove me to want more became a compelling desire to want more of God in my life. As this was a profound revelation for me, I realized God was giving me permission to shop (Search Him On Purpose) as much as I wanted. In the process I found the look I was searching to have! "I delight greatly in the LORD; my soul rejoices in my God. For he has clothed me with garments of salvation and arrayed me in a robe of righteousness, as a bridegroom adorns his head like a priest, and as a bride adorns herself with her jewels" (Psalm 61:10).

While I'm always keeping a sharp eye for great bargains and sales, when it comes to God's fashion, I won't settle for anything less than the best (and you shouldn't either) no ifs or buts about it! Here's the real deal in God's fashion:

Forgiving–Micah 7:18   Illuminating–Exodus 13:21

Absolute–Psalm 86:8–10   Omniscient–Daniel 2:20–22

Savior–Jude 1:24–25   Near–Psalm 145:13–20

Holy–Psalm 99:9

G*S.T.Y.L.E... has become a way of life reminding me God is some thing you live every day. In His fashion we have a source of hope and the promise of new life.

God saw all that he had made and it was very good. Is there something you live every day? How about God?

What's Your S.T.Y.L.E.?

I love to shop and I always look forward to seeing the new "in" styles for the season. Sometimes they're bold, and sometimes they're vibrant or calm, or cool and sophisticated, or even playful prints. Did you know God desires us to be styled in the attitudes, motives and characteristics that define His "in" style for all-season wear?

I see **S.T.Y.L.E.** as *some thing you live everyday*. With "you" in the middle, it *makes* it personal. Your personal style may reflect your manner of dress, the way you express yourself or your way of life.

Styles change through the years, but one style that never changes is the basic black dress. Long or short, long-sleeved or no sleeves, the basic black dress remains an ageless style. It coordinates with every color or print, and can be dressed up or down depending on the accessories used, looking good on every body type.

God's Word is like the basic black dress. It never changes. The long and short of it is, it was true yesterday, is true today and will be true tomorrow. It coordinates faith and works, and can be accessorized in church with praise and worship or comfortably dressed in Bible study.

I see Paul as a **S.T.Y.L.I.S.T.** (*some thing you live in simple truth*). He was fashioned in faith with the simple truth of Scripture. He lived it because he was a Pharisee. After being filled with

---

Stylist Advise:

Paul – "For I have learned to be content whatever the circumstances. I know what it is to be in need, and I know what it is to have plenty. I have learned the secret of being content in any and every situation, whether well fed or hungry, whether living in plenty or in want. I can do everything through him who gives me strength."

Philippians 4:11-13

Matthew – "If you believe, you will receive whatever you ask for in prayer."

Matthew 21:22

> Jesus – "I have told you these things, so that in me you may have peace. In this world you will have trouble. But take heart! I have overcome the world."
>
> John 16:33

the Holy Spirit (Acts 9), his eyes were fully opened to the truth, which fueled his passion for preaching the gospel to the Jews and gentiles. It became his *life* style.

How would you define your life style? Would you consider yourself a slave to fashion? Do you wear styles because they are the in fashion for the season, or are you a S.T.Y.L.I.S.T.? If you'd asked me that question a few years ago, I would have told you I was a slave to fashion; "We must pay more careful attention, therefore, to what we have heard, so that we do not drift away" (Hebrews 2:1). As my style has changed throughout the years, God's promises have become some thing I live everyday. I live knowing He is faithful. He promised to never to leave or forsake us. He promised things for my good and not for harm. We can live each day with joy and purpose knowing the faithfulness of God.

If you're not sure about your style, you can always start as I did, with the basic black dress (the Word of God). As I began to accessorize with praise and worship, and dress comfortably with Bible study, I found *my* personal style. I still love to look at all the new styles, but instead of changing to fit the current style, now I look for things that bring joy and purpose to the style I already have! Stay with me while I wow you with a new style to wear this season.

G*S.T.Y.L.E.!

Kind of catchy don't you think? I just love it. It makes me smile when I say it. Since God is always in fashion (you'll discover why

> **G*Style** — "Among the Gods is none like you, O Lord, nor are there any works like your works. All nations who you have made shall come and worship before you, O Lord, and shall glorify your name. For you are great, and do wondrous things; You alone are God."
>
> Psalm 86:8-10, NASB

I say that later on), you can probably figure out where I'm going with this. Okay...here's the wow part.

God is some thing you live everyday (G*S.T.Y.L.E.) because we find *grace* and *glory* in Him. We have His *gift* of salvation through faith with the *guiding* light of his truth. Through His *goodness* and *gentleness* we find comfort and are filled with His joy and peace.

Glorious, don't you think? Didn't I tell you? Are you smiling too? Don't all those "G" words just add passion to G*S.T.Y.L.E.? I'll bet you never thought of it that way. I didn't either. God just *gently* laid it on my heart to *give* to you. So now you have it, something new to wear today and everyday!

G*S.T.Y.L.E. is the basis for developing a passion for God's fashion. In addition to the "wow" that makes us smile, it is vertically and horizontally styled for us.

Vertical styling provides balance and order.

G—is God who comes first in our life.

*—is a star and represents the Holy Spirit. (Though stars aren't always visible, they are always present, just like the Holy Spirit.)

S—is the Savior.

t—is the cross. Can you see it?

y—is you, the reason the Savior died on the cross.

l—is the love God has for you.

e—is eternal life. What we have when we believe in Him.

Being horizontally styled adds meaning, motivation and purpose.

The Trinity [the meaning]: God the Father (G), the Holy Spirit (*) and the Savior (S) Jesus Christ [the motivation] who died on the cross (t) for you (y). Through his unconditional love for you [the purpose], you can live (l) eternally (e) with him in Heaven.

Be vertically and horizontally styled in God and you'll be fashionably dressed for every season!

"…And then take on an entirely new way of life—a God-fashioned life, a life renewed from the inside and working itself into your conduct as God accurately reproduces his character in you"

Ephesians 4: 22–24, MSG

The Passion

If passion were a color, it would be rich, bold and vivid. If it were a song, it would sing loudly and rejoice. I think life should be lived with passion.

Most of life is ordinary. Ordinary pays the bills, cleans the house, goes to work and keeps things on an even keel. Passion lives in the Kingdom. It doesn't worry about tomorrow, it rejoices in the blessings of today. It lives in the world but is not of the world. Passion runs deep.

> "For God so loved the world that He gave His only son, that whosoever believes in Him shall not perish but have everlasting life"
>
> John 3:16

Passion develops over time. It's born with desire, turns into action, and grows more as it matures. Passion resides in the body with legs to walk in the right direction and arms to reach out and hold. A heart pumping with excitement and a mind that believes if it can conceive it will achieve. It has a spirit that is inspired and uplifted. Passion is active. It doesn't just sit there; it gets up and gets going!

Passion isn't conceited or concerned with how silly it looks. It expresses itself in pure joy. Passion is innovative and inventive. It may start as curiosity and blossom into a life saving treatment or a hybrid vehicle or a cell phone. Passion is *pass*ed *on* to others. It shares its wisdom, hopes and dreams to pass on to the next generation.

Developing Passion

Passion can develop slowly like a seed planted in fertile soil growing strong and steady. It can move quickly to capture the moment and create memories, or remain steady when joined with one who shares your same passion. "As iron sharpens iron, so one man sharpens another" (Proverbs 27:17)

Sometimes God brings people together for the purpose of sharpening. My best friend, Lynnette, and I have shared many times of sharpening one another, but one time stands out most in my mind. Lynnette and I were in the same season of planting and being planted. We decided to go on a road trip to Williamsburg, Virginia, to spend three days clothing ourselves in Christ. We packed up our fashion guide, CDs, notebooks, DVDs and hit the road! I really didn't know what to expect, but I knew it would be wonderful. We prayed, cried, laughed and learned so much about God, and he gave us such revelation and understanding that we came back on fire for Him. It was an awesome time! I had never experienced "girlfriend" time like that before. Being so rooted in God together and equally yoked, we'd finish each other's sentences before the other could get the words out! Of course we did our share of shopping at the outlet stores (you knew we would), but this was an experience I'll never forget. I thank God for putting us together because he knew exactly what I needed to fuel my passion for him and in his infinite love for me; he made sure I received it!

Solomon had a passion for wisdom. In receiving it, he was given far more than he imagined, and had the wisdom to handle all he had. I'm not a fashion expert. I don't have a degree from any fashion design school, but I have a passion for God, to be fashioned in his Word, a need for his clothing, and to know his will for my life.

A Passion for Clothing

Since fashion is our discussion topic, I think it fitting we talk about clothing. Did you know our Fashion Guide has much to say about clothing?

- Clothing is what we put on our body and our spirit.

- Armor is used to protect the body from physical attacks and metaphorically used in Ephesians 6 to protect us from spiritual attacks.

- People tore their clothing in repentance.

- The cloth that veiled the Ark of the Covenant was torn from top to bottom when Jesus died.

- Clothing has power from on high. "And behold, I am sending forth the promise of My Father upon you; but you are to stay in the city until you are clothed with power from on high" (Luke 24:49, NASB).

Seven years ago I had a sincere desire to know Jesus. I'd attended Christian conferences with my church group and wanted the passion for Christ I'd seen demonstrated in the speakers, singers and audience. Knowing Christ is desire. Desiring to be clothed in Christ is passion. Passion for Christ requires taking off our old nature to put on newness of life in Him; "and to put on the new self, created to be like God in true righteousness and holiness" (Ephesians 4:24).

I know now that those speakers, singers and audience members weren't just caught up in the moment. They were clothed in Christ praising their new life in Him. I think passion for Christ is something you feel so deep inside you that causes such joy you can't contain it and it bursts out into rejoicing and praise.

Have you ever bought an outfit you couldn't wait to put on? You pull off the tags, put it on a hanger and just stare at it for a while. When morning comes, you quickly put it on and admire yourself in the mirror. You look different, like a new person. It makes you feel good just wearing it. You feel confident and happy. That's just an inkling of how you'll feel when passionately clothed in the LORD. Out of my desire to know Him, I can now confidently say I am passionately clothed in Christ Jesus.

"God proves to be good to the man who passionately waits, to the woman who diligently seeks" (Lamentations 3:25, MSG).

Do you desire to know Christ? Do you want to know His will for your life? If you answered yes, here are some words of inspiration for The Passion.

"Here's what I'm saying: Ask and you'll get; Seek and you'll find; Knock and the door will open" (Luke 11:9, MSG.)

"Your baptism in Christ was not just washing you up for a fresh start. It also involved dressing you in an adult faith wardrobe—Christ's life, the fulfillment of God's original promise" (Galatians 3:27, MSG)

"But what does it say? 'The word is near you; it is in your mouth and in your heart,' that is, the word of faith we are proclaiming: That if you confess with your mouth, 'Jesus is LORD,' and believe in your heart that God raised him from the dead, you will be saved. For it is with your heart that you believe and are justified, and it is with your mouth that you confess and are saved" (Romans 10:8–10).

A Passion for Worship

When thinking of worship, the first thing that comes to mind is church. While church is where we assemble for congregational worship, I think God desires us to worship Him in all areas of our life.

We demonstrate worship when we wake up in the morning, open our eyes and give God praise for seeing a new day. When he's the first thing we think about when faced with challenging circumstances and we look to Him for wisdom—that's worship. When we thank him for the blessings of the day or realize that life's lemons are meant to grow our faith and we praise Him for carrying us through—that's worship. Whenever we take the time to count our blessings or pray for others when God lays them on our heart—that's worshiping Him in obedience.

Passion gives us fresh ways for worship when we include God in our everyday life. I've experienced great times of fresh worship in teaching. Every time I commit to leading a ladies' ministry activity, God gives me fresh, fun ways to present His message. Whenever we seek ways to bring Christ into people's lives, He equips us with the tools we need to carry it out.

As a Sunday school teacher of adults, it's always challenging to get people to understand how relative biblical truths apply to the life issues we face today. I find relating life experiences that parallel the study lesson sparks conversation in sharing, and adds passion to our worship time. I think now you fully understand the motivation behind The Passion. Later on, I will take you on a shopping trip. While you passionately wait, let's learn about The Fashion.

The Fashion

I love word search puzzles. When you first look at them, all you
see is a bunch of letters that don't seem to make sense. After
looking at them from different angles, the words seem to jump
out from the page!

When you look at fashion, what do you see? Most of us just see a word. I bet if you look hard enough, you'll see God in fashion. The mystery in solving puzzles is to look for the connection to find the answer. If you look for *God,* you won't find it in fashion. You have to look a little deeper. There's the *F*ather who *A*pproved the *S*on to save us from our sins, the *H*oly Spirit to guide and comfort us with *I*nfinite love *O*ffering *N*ew life.

Now do you see God in fashion? It isn't obvious at first, but when you really look for God, you'll find Him. Another thing you'll find in fashion are the first and last letters of the Greek alphabet. Can you guess what they are? That's right! The Alpha and Omega; the beginning and end. Although "a" isn't the first letter in fashion, it comes after the Father, and "o" isn't the end, it's new life!

Though words may seem to be hidden among a lot of disconnected letters, God is never hidden from us, nor is He disconnected. When we focus our eyes on Him, we'll find He's always in fashion!

Fashion...Forward.

"Your truth never goes out of fashion; it's as up-to-date as the earth when the sun comes up."

Psalm 119:90, MSG

Common Sense for Fashion Sense

I think fashion sense comes from knowing what fashions look good on you. I think it is also inherent to our nature. The

Designer (the originator of fashion) indwells us with good fashion sense.

> "For since the creation of the world God's invisible qualities—his eternal power and divine nature—have been clearly seen, being understood from what has been made, so that men are without excuse"
>
> Romans 1:20

Our Fashion Guide gives many illustrations of people with good fashion sense who've made bad fashion choices based on advice they received from fashion consultants who didn't have their best interest at heart. We find one such case in Genesis.

There was a handsome young apprentice who worked closely with the Designer in his studio. The apprentice studied with and learned from the Designer. The Designer had the very best fashions made of the finest quality, construction and style. The apprentice foolishly thought he could create the same fashions as the Designer. His arrogance and envy got the best of him and soon he and the Designer had a falling out and the Designer threw him out of his studio. It was then the apprentice decided to open his own studio to create designer knock offs.

While the apprentice was busy putting his studio together, Eve was shopping at the prestigious Garden Mall. The Designer created the mall filled with the finest fashions. As he walked with her on a tour, he told her she could shop in any of the stores, but she was forbidden to shop at the Tree of Life store. Eve was totally content shopping at all the other stores. They had many beautiful fashions that she didn't mind skipping over one.

As Eve was sitting down to lunch at the food court, the apprentice came and sat down beside her. He's very fashionably dressed and compliments her on her fashion style. He tells her he's a fashion consultant personally taught by the Designer and is launching a new line of designer fashions. He invites her to try them at the Tree of Life store. Remembering what the Designer had said, Eve tells the apprentice she's forbidden to shop there. The apprentice tells her the Designer doesn't want her to shop there because if she does, it'll prove she has the same fashion sense as him, and she'll be able to re-create His fashions herself.

Eve expresses her unwillingness to walk to the end of the mall to shop in the Tree of Life store. The apprentice thinks for a moment, cleverly reaches into his designer portfolio and pulled out his Apple laptop computer. He tells her she can shop at the store online. He convinced her she'll show off her good fashion sense and all she'll have to do is simply type her user ID and password. He even offered her instant credit! Eve decides to look at the Tree of Life fashions, so she enters her user ID and password. As soon as she presses the <Enter> key, she instantly realized what she'd done. By shopping at the Tree of Life store, she's chosen to relinquish her wardrobe of innocence, glory and splendor for garments of guilt, shame, pain, and sin.

Even though Eve had good fashion sense, she received bad advice from the apprentice who was more concerned about selling his knock-off fashions than he was in helping her look her best.

Later on I'll take you shopping to one of my favorite fashion boutiques, but there's one rule about shopping there; they only take the Master's Card. Since I want you to be able to join me, let's take a detour to the Bank of The Almighty and apply for the card.

I think designer fashions are an investment. The Designer allows us to have them at his expense. He gives us credit (the Master's Card) for coming to Him for all we need and desire in life. All we have to do is apply to be approved. Once approved,

He gives us accounts in which to invest wisely and to plan for the future.

The Master's Card
Est. in the Bank of The Almighty
"In God We Trust"

What does it mean to trust in God? (Proverbs 3: 4-5)

To trust in God means we enter into a covenant relationship with Him (Colossians 2:2-7) with a child-like faith, accepting Him as Lord (Matthew 10:14). The covenant relationship has entitlements that allow us to set our sights on the rich treasures and joys of heaven (Colossians 3:1). It gives us direction, letting God become involved in our decisions (Colossians 3:1, 16).

It's important to know and understand about trust because "banking" it means we put what we have into something that has meaning and purpose (Colossians 3:10). Banking our trust in God increases our interest rate, gives us instant access, profit sharing, investment banking, stocks and free gifts.

Interest Rates – Market predictors indicate that your interest rate will go up!

As your interest in material things for happiness decreases (Colossians 3:2), your interest in eternal happiness will be on the rise. It's compounded daily, as you trust God to walk with you in each day's fluctuations (Colossians 2:6).

Be sure to check your interest rate to balance your life by putting your trust in God!

Instant Access – You have a joint account (living in vital union with Christ) that gives you 24/7 voice activation (prayer – Nehemiah 1:5), with voice recognition (John 10:14) for guidance, service, comfort and forgiveness.

Profit Sharing – You are fully vested, which means you have instant access to the Almighty. You don't have to stand in line or fill out any forms. You simply come, just as you are, and ask Him to come into your heart.

Long-term Ability (there's no "dis" in this ability!):

- the assurance of forgiveness
- freedom from evil desires
- happiness (joy)
- personal growth
- thankfulness to God
- ability through the power of God that wouldn't be possible on our own.

Long-term Care –The provider will increase your benefits (while paying your premiums) as you mature (in faith).

Life Assurance – Your name is written in the Book of Life!
Prophet Sharing (through His Word you'll have access to His greatest representatives) – Our Fashion Guide tells of many prophets who spoke by the power of the Spirit preaching the message of God to help us grow in the Lord. Prophecy (preaching) is meant to be shared to communicate God's Word to us providing correction, insight, warning and encouragement. Some spoke through visions (like Ezekiel); some spoke through dreams

(like Daniel); and some shared The Revelation (like John). As you read, study, and understand truth revealed through prophecy, share your knowledge with others. By sharing the truth, we all profit!

Investment Banking – When you bank your trust in God, it's vital to invest wisely.

Be sure to choose profitable allocations:
- Banking your trust in God wipes out fear and gives you a secure future.
- Investing time in learning God's will for your life will give you guaranteed interest!
- Deposit hope into your checking account to prevent early withdrawls.
- Allocate equal portions of compassion, kindness, gentleness and goodness into others for a balanced portfolio.
- Keep a minimum daily balance of love, hope and faith in your checking account.

A Living Will – I view a Living Will as living in the Will of God. It's about seeking Him and finding His will for your life. Having a will without living in the Light is spiritual darkness. A living will exists in the here and now and is more precious (valuable) when we willingly commit ourselves completely to Him. He gives us free will. To choose Him is a Living Will!

"He will give eternal life to those who patiently do the will of God, seeking for the unseen glory and honor and eternal life that he offers."

Romans 2:7 (TKB)

Stocks & Bonds – There's stock in the trust we place in God. Faith, hope and love will mature overtime the longer you hold onto them.

- Certificates of Deposit (God's promises) – Secured in faith and guaranteed in writing (look for them in your Fashion Guide).
- Bond daily with the Master and put stock in His Word.
- Bond with others in Christian love. It's the glue that bonds us together (Colossians 2:2).

Entitlements – When you put your trust in God, you are approved to receive his Gift Card:

- There's no grace period to receiving his Grace.
- No deferred billing in his Mercy, he expresses it to us daily.
- No annual percentage rate on God's Favor.

- No shipping charges to receive His Forgiveness of sin; only handling!
- No late payment fee to receive Salvation.

Now that we know what we have in our trust, let's apply for the Master's Card. It's as easy as ABC.

__ I admit that I am a sinner.
"For all have sinned, and fall short of the glory of God."

Romans 3:23

__ I believe that Jesus is God the Son who paid the wages of my sin.

"For the wages of sin is death; but the gift of God is eternal life through Jesus Christ our Lord."

Romans 6:23

___ I call upon God. I confess with my mouth that Jesus is Lord. I believe in my heart that God raised Jesus from death and I am saved.

"For if you tell others with your own mouth that Jesus Christ is Lord, and believe in your heart that God raised him from the dead, you will be saved."

Romans 10:9 (TKB)

Signature: _____

Date: _____

Congratulations! You're Approved!

Here's your confirmation of acceptance:

He has given us both his promise and his oath, two things we can completely count on, for it is impossible for God to tell a lie. Now all those who flee to him to save them can take new courage when they hear such assurances from God; now they can know without a doubt that he will give them the salvation he has promised them. This certain hope of being saved is a strong and trustworthy anchor for our souls, connecting us with God himself behind the sacred curtains of heaven, where Christ has gone ahead to plead for us from his position as our High Priest with the honor and rank of Melchizedek [king of righteousness].

Hebrews 6:18–20, TLB

Now that you are an official member (approved) in the body of Christ, be sure to have your Master's Card with you at all times. "Our bodies have many parts, but the many parts make up only one body when they are all put together. So it is with the 'body' of Christ" (1 Corinthians 12:12 TLB).

It is *C*hrist's *A*pproval, *R*ighteous and *D*ivine!

I hope you profited from our little detour. I know I did. It gave me a chance to check my balance, watch my interest rate, see a return on my investments and reaffirm my trust is in the right place!

Now we have everything we need for our shopping trip. At the appointed time, go down Free Will Blvd. Turn right at the corner of Decision Street and Salvation Way. There you will see the Light. On track 7 you'll find me waiting by the train. Be sure to bring your Master's Card with you. It is your ticket to ride the Almighty Express. See you soon!

Fashions That Stand the Test of Time

One fashion I have desired to wear is patience. While some wear patience well like my husband, Phillip, my impetuous nature doesn't let me stand still long enough to put it on!

Patience

I think that in order to wear patience, it has to be tested and inspected. Have you ever seen the "Wear Dated" tag on certain garments? Wear Dated means the garment is tested many times under certain conditions and inspected to see how well it holds up. I've heard people say, "Be careful what you wish for, you just might get it!" I think it's especially true of patience. If you pray for it, it will be tested! You don't get to choose under which conditions it will be tested. That's God's job and He will inspect us to see how well we hold up. "And patience develops strength of character in us and helps us to trust God more each time we use it until finally our hope and faith makes us strong and steady" (Romans 5:4, TLB).

I admire this fashion for its fabric content (strength in character), craftsmanship (trust in God) and quality construction (strong and steady) and I can look forward to wearing it more and more each day!

Faith

Some fashions, like faith, are worn at an early age and grow as we mature. Job was fashioned in faith at an early age and it grew in him. His faith definitely had a Wear Dated tag. It was tested under harsh conditions of loss, deep affliction, isolation and sadness, but he proved his faith could stand the test of time. God approved Job's faithfulness and restored what was lost, and adorned him in abundance.

Hope

Hope is one fashion that stands the test of time through repeated washings in cold water to keep it from fading. David found cold-water washings of desperation, despair and depression kept his hope from fading. Water, even when cold is cleansing. Through cleansing we find the hope that retains it's color (joy). To keep colors from fading in the wash, we use a color guard as protection from harsh detergents. Hope should be worn during times when we live in cold, sometimes cruel situations to let God protect us from harsh conditions to retain the joy we have in Him. "But LORD, you are my shield, my glory and my only hope" (Psalm 3:3, TLB)

Courage

Some fashions are flame resistant like the ones worn by Shadrah, Meshach and Abednego. Their fashions were tested for durability in the fiery furnace. They refused the decree of king Nebuchad-nessar to fall down and worship his image made of gold. Cour-age is the fashion of choice when refusing to compromise our beliefs even when it's not the "popular" thing to do "Shadrach, Meshach, and Abednego replied, "O Nebuchadnezzar, we do not need to defend ourselves before you. If we are thrown into the blazing furnace, the God whom we serve is able to save us. He will rescue us from your power, Your Majesty. But even if he doesn't, we want to make it clear to you, Your Majesty, that we will never serve your gods or worship the gold statue you have set up" (Daniel 3:16–18, NLT).

While popularity may get you noticed, it's durability that stands the test of time. "All the important people, the government leaders and king's counselors, gathered around to examine them and discovered that the fire hadn't so much as touched the three men—not a hair singed, not a scorch mark on their clothes, not even the smell of fire on them!" (Daniel 3:27, MSG).

These are just four of the time-tested fashions found in our Fashion Guide. There are many more and I encourage you to take time to study the wisdom and experience put into these fashions.

Brand Name Fashions

B.Y.O.F.G–Bring Your Own Fashion Guide and come with me to find some Brand Name fashions! If I told you there are many brand name fashions in our Fashion Guide, would you believe me?

Brand names are often known by one-word names like "Levi's." Levi's (Levites) were a tribe of men who were special servants of God (Israel's priests) in the temple.

Ever heard of "Liz"? She was the mother of John the Baptist. The angel Gabriel foretold this good news, "…Your wife Elizabeth will bear you a son, and you are to give him the name John. He will be a joy and delight to you, and many will rejoice because of his birth, for he will be great in the sight of the LORD" (Luke 1:13–15).

What about "Tommy"? Also known as doubting Thomas. He was one of Jesus' disciples who needed to see Jesus' wounds to believe He was truly the savior resurrected from the dead.

"Jordan" is the name of a famous basketball player, but is

also the place where Jesus was baptized. "Then Jesus came from Galilee to the Jordan to be baptized by John" (Matthew 3:13).

Brand name fashions are sought after because we recognize and relate to the quality and style of the person known by their signature brand. Often we find the identity of brand names through catch phases to easily recognize them. Who do you think of when I say "a man after God's own heart"? Do you think of David? How about "the wisdom of Solomon"? That was easy.

Brand names are also known by titles like "The Comforter" a.k.a. the Holy Spirit, or "The Savior," which is Jesus Christ, or "The Ten Commandments" brought down from the mountain by Moses.

Brand names can also be recognized by signature colors. If I were to say "A coat of many colors" would you recognize him? Joseph of course. How about the sweet smell of "Passion"? (One of my personal favorites!) The cologne bottle just happens to be purple (my favorite color), and purple symbolizes royalty.

Does the brand name "Timberland" remind you of the wilderness fashions worn by John the Baptist? He grew up in the wilderness, led many people in Israel to Christ, and preceded Christ with the same power and spirit as the prophet Elijah.

What about boating? Do you think of "Nautica"? Noah was six hundred years old when he went into the boat (with his family and a male and female of every kind of animal and bird) to escape the flood, and he did everything the LORD had told him to do. The sky opened up like windows and rain poured down for forty days and nights without stopping.

These are just a few of the many brand name fashions. Be sure to keep looking in our Fashion Guide to find many more!

Counterfeit Fashions

"Watch for false prophets. They come to you in sheep's clothing but inwardly they are ferocious wolves. By their fruit you will recognize them" (Matthew 7:15–16)

One way to challenge "truth in advertising" is to recognize counterfeit fashions from Designer originals. Counterfeit fashions always have clues that reveal their true value. If it's too good to be true or has hidden motives attached, then it's probably fake.

> **Fashion Tip #1**
> Accessorize your faith with the belt of truth buckled around your waist. (Ephesians 6:14)

As our fashion sense matures, we'll be able to distinguish quality in designer originals from counterfeits. So what makes up the quality?

Designer originals always have a trademark indicating it's an original. They always have a care label.

Having designer originals are important. When Christ returns we will be recognized as belonging to him. "Wait! Don't do anything yet, hurt neither the earth nor sea nor trees until we have placed the seal of God upon the foreheads of his servants" (Revelation 7:3, NLT). Those wearing Christ's signature will be gathered to meet Him and those wearing counterfeit fashions will be fooled by counterfeit miracles, signs and wonders. "The coming of the lawless one will be in accordance with the work of Satan displayed in all kinds of counterfeit miracles, signs and wonders, and in every sort of evil that deceives those who are perishing. They perish because they refused to love the truth and so be saved" (2 Thessalonians 2:10).

There will be times we may mistake counterfeit fashions for Designer originals. Counterfeit fashions will look like the original. They will appear to have the same quality construction and style. Some may even claim their fashions have the Designer's Signature logo, "He will exalt himself and defy everything that people call god and every object of worship. He will even sit in the temple of God, claiming that he himself is God," (2 Thessalonians 2:4, NLT). But we'll be able to recognize them as fake; " Don't be fooled by what they say. For that day will not come until there is a great rebellion against God and the man of lawlessness is revealed—the one who brings destruction" (2 Thessalonians 2:3, NLT).

By carefully inspecting the care label you'll become a savvy shopper of designer originals. "…from the beginning God chose you to be saved through the sanctifying work of the Spirit and through belief in the truth. He called you to this through our gospel, that you might share in the glory of our LORD Jesus Christ" (2 Thessalonians 2:13–14).

Care labels are important because they give us instructions on how to properly care for Designer originals. When we follow them, we ensure our fashions will last forever (eternally). They will stand up against any adverse conditions.

A savvy shopper of designer originals always does their homework. They read and study the Fashion Guide to know where and how to find Designer originals. They talk to others who have them to learn more about quality, style and value. They determine if the price they'll pay for the Designer original is worth it.

Careful inspection will prove their worth. If it's constructed with fabrics like self-serving, envy and fear woven in—it's a fake. If it is manufactured in a place other than the Designer's studio—it's a fake. If it is not constructed according to the Designers perfect instruction on salvation and grace—a fake. If the care label instructs us to be self-indulgent regardless of who it hurts—it's a fake.

The moment we determine we've discovered a fake, we should rebuke the counterfeit designer with a loud voice to alert others so they don't make the same mistake; "Take no part in the worthless pleasures of evil and darkness, but instead, rebuke and expose them" (Ephesians 5:11, TLB).

Designer originals are recognized by the Designer's trademark signature of Truth. Love, joy, peace, patience, kindness, gentleness, goodness, faithfulness and self-control are carefully woven into everyone who wears these fashions. Constructed with the highest quality, the care label instructs us to love others as ourselves, to forgive those who trespass against us in the same way we have been forgiven by the Father, to run from temptation, and to be delivered from evil.

"This is how you can recognize the Spirit of God. Every spirit that acknowledges that Jesus Christ has come in the flesh is from God" (1 John 4:2).

Don't be fooled by false advertising. Look for the clues that tell whether or not you have a true designer original. Inspect the construction, design, style, care label and signature. When you know without a doubt you have a designer original, be assured you have the very best!

It's In The Bag!

Designer bags are all the rage. You see them coming down fashion runways and carried by many famous people. They are the "in" fashion accessory.

While I have a variety of designer bags, there's one I have that outshines all the rest. It's my G*S.T.Y.L.E. bag! Do you have one for yourself? I guess before I ask you that question its only fair that I explain what it is. There are handbags and shoulder bags and bags with no handles, but a G*S.T.Y.L.E. bag is all that. It's *b*elievers *a*biding in *G*od.

> But as for you, the anointing (the sacred appointment, the unction) which you received from Him abides [permanently] in you; [so] then you have no need that anyone should instruct you. But just as His anointing teaches you concerning everything and is true and is no falsehood, so you must abide in (live in, never depart from) Him [being rooted in Him, knit to Him], just as [His anointing] has taught you [to do].
>
> 1 John 2:27, TAB

While I admit I'm not always faithful to abide in God, (obey, dwell, live in), He is faithful in abiding in me. You might ask why I chose this bag over my others. I asked myself the same question as I have learned to be open and aware of God's presence in my life.

Have you heard the expression "it's in the bag"? It means

that whatever you're counting on, you have the assurance you will have it. You might also ask what it is I find in this bag that makes it so special.

Have you ever visited a Designer bag store? Where do you find most of the exclusive sought-after designer bags? Locked behind glass. They can be seen artfully displayed in glass cabinets. While designer bags are "my thing", they aren't of much use to me sitting behind glass. I can't touch them or see what's inside. I have to settle for admiring them from a distance until I ask someone to take one out.

As you admire the bags sitting behind the glass, take a moment and look to your right. You might not have noticed this bag sitting on the table. Do you see it? Yes. That's the one.

The shoulder straps are draped over the cross-shaped display and there are tiny nails attached to keep it in place.

> "But whenever someone turns to the LORD, the veil is taken away. For the LORD is the Sprit, and wherever the Spirit of the LORD is, there is freedom".
>
> 2 Corinthians 3:16–17

You take notice that this bag is not sitting behind glass. It's out in the open! So you move toward it to get a closer look.

"Since this new way gives us such confidence, we can be very bold" (2 Corinthians 3:12, NLT).

You lean forward to see the brilliant light illuminating from inside the bag.

> "For God, who said 'Let there be light in the darkness', has made this light shine in our hearts so we could know the glory of God that is seen in the face of Jesus Christ".
>
> (2 Corinthians 4:6, NLT).

Just as Jesus invited Thomas to come and touch his nail-pierced hands, He invites us to come and touch Him.

With glassy eyes, you look inside the bag. You find it lined with the glory of the LORD! The pockets are full of His grace and mercy. While you open your eyes a little wider to see what's deep inside, you notice the inscription on a piece of leather sewn in the lining that simply says "I Am."

"So all of us who have had the veil removed can see and reflect the glory of the LORD" (2 Corinthians 3:18, NLT).

Do you see now why I choose this bag over all the others?

"So we don't look at the troubles [the things behind the glass] we can see now, rather we fix our gaze on the things that cannot be seen. For the things we see now will soon be gone, but the things we cannot see will last forever" (2 Corinthians 4:18, NLT).

God invites us to touch and be touched by him. From a distance we can only see the Light. Up close (abiding) we can *feel* the Light! There's nothing standing in our way to keep us from Him. The veil was removed for us to come directly to him. He's right here…if we abide in him.

Though I can't physically see my **G*S.T.Y.L.E.** bag, I know where it is, and it goes with me wherever I go. We carry bags to hold the essentials we take with us each day, to access them when needed. All we have to do is reach in to find what we're looking for. Sometimes we have to hunt a little, but it's always "in the bag."

So, what's in the bag for you?

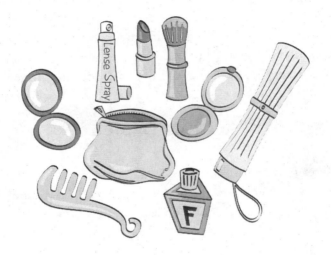

Do you find it lined with possibilities and pockets of inspiration? Do you find the lipstick that speaks the truth of God's Word? Do you see the comb that neatens out the messiness of life and sets our paths straight? Do you see the compact mirror that reflects God's glory in you, and the wallet so full of blessings it can't be zipped to keep them from overflowing? Do you see the foundation makeup that covers sin and gives us an even-toned righteous walk with God, or the blush of joy that adds color to our life? Or perhaps you've found the glass cleaner that removes the dust from our eyes so we can better see with our "Son" glasses on. Do you find the umbrella (the Holy Spirit) of comfort and-protection when you open up to Him, or the peace that covers us when we are in the will of God?

Now that you are intimately familiar with the G*S.T.Y.L.E. bag, are you willing to carry it wherever you go?

If you're not sure, look again at those exclusive designer bags displayed behind glass and see if you can guess what's inside. Then look right at the G*S.T.Y.L.E.. bag and know without a doubt what's inside. Know that the veil was removed so you can get closer to the truth and get it directly from the source (God). Distance doesn't make the heart grow fonder. It separates us from the heart of God. Believers, abide in God. It's in the bag!

Fashion Basics

I consider fashion basics to be the things we wear for everyday use. Basics are built for comfort, purpose, style and durability. The following are seven fashion basics for you.

- Fashion T's

- The Layered Look

- Spring Collection

- Intimate Apparel

- Workout Gear

- Summer's Top 7–The Season's Must-Haves to keep Cool when the Heat is on

- Fall Fashion Forecast–Reality Dressing.

Fashion Tip #2: Fashion Measuring
- Be sure to measure your faith, taking into account room for growth.
- When you put on the breastplate of righteousness and the belt of truth, you want it form fitting (in God) and comfortable.
- Measure your shoe size to have good footing in your walk with God (Easy Spirit!)
- When measuring your waist don't waste time worrying. Cut down your intake of anxiety and insecurity and re-measure. I'll bet you'll find a reduction in your waist!

Fashion T's
Style with Support

Fashion T's are top-notch fashions for built-in lift and figure-flattering shape-enhancement. V-neck T's are virtuous (very figure-flattering!). Scoop neck T's are very well rounded. Square-neck T's are straight and to the point, and the softest T's speak wisdom and truth with a gentle spirit. Use the following fashion T's for stylish ways to look your best!

- Monday–*Think* positive. "As a man (or woman) thinks, so he (she) is."

- Tuesday–*Talk* to God. He wants a relationship with you.

- Wednesday–*Take time* to pray.

- Thursday–*Thank* God for your blessings.

- Friday–*Test* the scriptures. Read your Fashion Guide.

- Saturday–*Teach* one, reach one for God.

- Sunday–*Turn* away from sin and turn toward the Father.

The Layered-Look
Fashion in a Minute

The layered look is a great style to wear. It's easy to put together and can be very fashionable. Create this look using 2 Peter 1:5–7 (HCSB) as your guide. "For this very reason, make every effort to supplement your faith with goodness, goodness with knowledge, knowledge with self-control, self-control with endurance, endurance with godliness, godliness with brotherly affection, and brotherly affection with love."

Spring Collection
Spring Forward into the Colors of Faith

Spring is the time of year to set our clock ahead one hour. I especially like this time because it gives me more time in the Son!

When I was little my dad told me I saw the world through rose-colored glasses. While I think it was true back then, now that I'm older I try to see more through "Son" glasses! While they're not rose-colored, they are colored in faith, and to get the true effect you need to wear your own Son glasses. Having said that, go get yours and meet me back here to look at the fashion colors in our Spring Collection.

GREEN–This color of faith grows deeper over time. You'll find variations like ivy, moss, lime, clover and grass that grow with plenty of water and lots of sunshine. Our faith grows and gets deeper over time when we have the Living Water of Truth and the light of the Son. Green symbolizes new life in Christ.

"You need to know, friends, that thanking God over and over for you is not only a pleasure; it's a must. We have to do it. Your faith is growing phenomenally; your love for each other is developing wonderfully. Why, it's only right that we give thanks" (2 Thessalonians 1:3, msg).

RED–Be bold; wear red! This color of faith has in it *r*edemption, *e*verlasting life and *d*ivine grace. Red also symbolizes Jesus' blood that was shed for you.

"But now in Christ Jesus you who once were far away have been brought near through the blood of Christ" (Ephesians 2:13).

BLUE–Tropical blues are the watercolors of faith like sky, aqua, ocean and river. It symbolizes baptism in Christ that cleanses and washes sin away.

"Peter replied, "Repent and be baptized, every one of you, in the name of Jesus Christ for the forgiveness of your sins. And you will receive the gift of the Holy Spirit" (Acts 2:38).

WHITE–Crisp...Clean...Pure. White is the absence of color just like our sins when they are forgiven. They are washed, hung on the line and dried in the Son.

"I, even I, am he who blots out your transgressions, for my own sake, and remembers your sins no more" (Isaiah 43:25)

ORANGE–Orange has the mystic power of the Son, the miracles of life that can only be explained by faith. This color of faith symbolizes the power of the Holy Spirit.

"I baptize you with water for repentance. But after me will come one who is more powerful than I, whose sandals I am not fit to carry. He will baptize you with the Holy Spirit and with fire" (Matthew 3:11).

PURPLE–The passion of Christ. It brings to mind the passionflower and the fact that we are heirs to the Kingdom. It symbolizes the crown of life placed on us because of our faith in Christ.

"He redeems you from hell—saves your life! He crowns you with love and mercy—a paradise crown" (Psalm 103:4, MSG).

Blast from the Past
Passionflower is also called Maypop. Spanish explorers in Peru discovered it in 1569. They saw the flowers as symbolic of the passion of Christ and a sign of Christ's approval from their efforts. Today, passionflower is displayed as a symbol of faith.

You might ask what "Victorious Secret" has to do with intimate apparel (besides sounding like a familiar brand name!). I think it can be summed up in a song.

"O Victory in Jesus, My Savior forever. He sought me and bought me with his redeeming love. He loved me ere I knew him and all my love is due Him. He plunged me to victory, beneath the cleansing flood."

Sound familiar? It is a hymn I've sung many times that always brings me joy.

Jesus said, "I am the good shepherd; I know my sheep and my sheep know me" (John 10:14). This is a statement of truth demonstrating the intimate relationship between the Creator and his creation (us).

Intimate apparel is what goes on underneath to add shape and definition. I would consider faith part of our intimate apparel because it is shaped on the belief that God is who He claims to be and is defined by the way we live or lives (our **G*S.T.Y.L.E.**). "The fundamental fact of existence is that this trust in God, this faith, is the firm foundation under everything that makes life worth living. It's our handle on what we can't see" (Hebrews 11:1, MSG).

The victorious secret is we don't have to hide ourselves from God. He knows us intimately (He even knows the number of hairs on our head!). He knows all of our faults and weaknesses, and yet He still loves us! Because he knows us intimately, we can freely go to him for anything.

Because we are made in the form of God (in His image) we

Victorious Secret #1:
Prayer. "But when you pray, go into your room, close the door and pray to your Father, who is unseen. Then your Father, who sees what is done in secret, will reward you." Matthew 6:6

---

have shape and definition in Him. (Madenform—get it? Just a little intimate apparel humor for you!)

I think intimate apparel resides within the heart (Cross Your Heart—I couldn't resist!). It's where our emotions and our desires live. It's where love grows and our spirit connects with the Holy Spirit for guidance and comfort. It's where belief comes alive. "….and believe in your heart that God raised him [Jesus] from the dead, you will be saved" (Romans 10:9, NLT).

I think Paul's words describe the passion of an intimate relationship with Christ:

Do you think anyone is going to be able to drive a wedge between us and Christ's love for us? There is no way! Not trouble, not hard times, not hatred, not hunger, not homelessness, not bullying threats, not backstabbing, not even the worst sins listed in Scripture. I'm absolutely convinced that nothing—nothing living or dead, angelic or demonic, today or tomorrow, high or low, thinkable or unthinkable—absolutely nothing can get between us and God's love because of the way that Jesus our Master has embraced us.

Romans 8:35, 38–39 (MSG

Well, I guess it really isn't a secret after all. You probably knew it all along, but you have to admit, it made for a great attention-getting title, a song to put in your heart, and some truth to add shape and definition to your style. Victorious, don't you think?

Workout Gear

When it comes to workout fashions, quality is key. Always look for quality fabrics that are durable, stretch and breathe, that won't bind, but move with you. Spandex/cotton blend is a two-way stretch fabric that moves with us when we exercise. God moves with us when we exercise our faith in him. He walks with us when we witness to others. He gives us just the right words to say. Often times I find myself in conversation with someone and the words just seem to flow from my mouth. When I think back on what I said, I can't always remember. That's God; that's two-way stretch.

Spandex/cotton is also breathable to keep the body cooled when we exercise. Our Fashion Guide is God-breathed. When we exercise continually in God's Word, he breathes understanding into us. Like one of my favorite hymns says, "How do I know? Because the Bible tells me so."

I have a set of aqua weights (dumbbells) I take with me when

I travel so I can workout. They are made of durable vinyl that collapses and fits easily into my suitcase. I simply fill them with water and attach them to the bar and they become the

weight. I think the aqua weights provide a great analogy for us to think about when we workout. We are the vinyl container and the Living Water (God's Word) is poured into us; it adds the weight of God's truth. What we use to workout with makes us strong in the LORD.

Summer's Top 7—The Season's Must-Haves to keep Cool when the Heat is on

"Blessed is the man who perseveres under trial, because when he has stood the test, he will receive the crown of life that God has promised to those who love him"

James 1:12

I included the Summer's Top 7 season must-haves in our Fashion Basics because we need some cool looks when our emotions heat up. When we learn how to adjust the thermostat when our temperature rises, we will always look cool in G*S.T.Y.L.E..

Truth: We experience times when we react to a situation or circumstance that leads us to say or do things in the "heat of the moment" we regret. When dealing with anger, worry, stress, fear, impatience, insecurity and bitterness (the Top 7), we need to be reminded to use good fashion sense in combination with cool wisdom from our Fashion Guide to ensure we have the proper temperature setting for looking cool and feeling refreshed when the heat is on!

1. When anger flares up, put on a wide-brimmed hat made of Son-washed, breathable fabric.

Some of us are like firecrackers. We flare up, shoot off (our mouths) and then cool down quickly. Some burn slowly, like on a stove, with steady rising heat. In either case, the outcome is the same. Neither is worse than the other, and anger always carries consequences, usually regret. Uncontrolled anger can lead to the death of a friendship, relationship or partnership. For this reason, we need a wide-brimmed hat to put a lid on our anger and cool off a hot head. When anger turns into a heat wave, we have a melt down. We don't think about where we are, what we're saying or who will be affected. We don't think at all! A covering made with Son-washed, breathable fabric (Christ's nature) provides protection from the scorching heat of anger. "Then the LORD said to Cain, 'Why are you angry? Why is your face downcast? If you do what is right, will you not be accepted? But if you do not do what is right, sin is crouching at your door; it desires to have you, but you must master it'" (Genesis 4:6–7). Mastering anger is a cool look to have. You can appreciate the wisdom (what the Son gives us) in thinking first before acting.

"I will instruct you and teach you in the way you should go.
I will counsel you and watch over you"

Psalm 32:8

"But now you must rid yourselves of all such things as these: anger, rage, malice, slander, and filthy language from your lips".

Colossians 3:8

2. If worry is heating you up inside, get "Dressed to Chill (out!)."

> Don't fret or worry. Instead of worrying, pray. Let petitions and praises shape your worries into prayers, letting God know your concerns. Before you know it, a sense of God's wholeness, everything coming together for good, will come and settle you down. It's wonderful what happens when Christ displaces worry at the center of your life.
>
> Philippians 4:6–7 (MSG)

3. If you find you're hot and bound by being dressed in stress, then less is best. Put on relaxed-fit stretch jeans. Relaxed-fit for ease of comfort and ample room for circulation with just enough stretch that won't get bent out of shape when you do!

When I was young (and much slimmer!), tight jeans were in style. You had to lie down on the bed to put your jeans on. The problem with tight jeans is they feel fine when lying down, but have no give when you get up! You can walk, but you can't bend over or sit down without inhaling first; and God help you if you sneeze! I think stress is like tight jeans. It has no give. It gets tighter and more uncomfortable when you over schedule, bend to pressure, and over obligate yourself. Because there's no give, the only way to get out of stress is to take it off!

"When anxiety was great within me, your consolation brought joy to my soul" (Psalm 94:19).

4. Prevent overexposure to fear by putting on your "Son" visor! Being exposed to fear heats up our insecurity and paranoia. It lies to us and makes us doubt. Our Son advisor tells us to fear not and trust in Him. Calm your fear with truth of the Spirit. "For you did not receive a spirit that makes you a slave to fear, but you received the Spirit of Sonship. And by him we cry 'Abba, Father'" (Romans 8:15).

"For I am the Lord, your God, who takes hold of your right hand and says to you, do not fear; I will help you".

Isaiah 41:13

5. When your patience is running short, put on a cool pair of shorts.

Have short dialogs with God! Turn away from your circumstances and turn your attention to him. He may be patiently waiting for you to come to him for a short answer to a question your have, or with some short wisdom on how to handle a situation; or short bursts of inspiration that would not have been realized with a short-temper.

"Be still before the Lord and wait patiently for him; do not fret when men succeed in their ways, when they carry out their wicked schemes".

Psalm 37:7

"Wait for the Lord, be strong and take heart and wait for the Lord!".

63

Psalm 27:14

6. When the pressure of insecurity heats up, put on your capris to walk confidently in the Lord.

I think insecurity is a lack of confidence. Without confidence, we have doubt and trouble making clear decisions. Indecisiveness can literally stop us in our tracks. It's important that we are confident in what we believe and believe in what we are confident about. When we believe without a doubt that God has a plan for our life, we can confidently walk in him.

"'For I know the plans I have for you,' declares the LORD, 'plans to prosper you and not to harm you, plans to give you hope and a future'."

Jeremiah 29:11

Trust in the LORD leads to open doors of understanding for us to see and follow him through.

"Trust in the LORD with all your heart and lean not on your

own understanding; in all your ways acknowledge him and he will make your paths straight."

Proverbs 3:5–6

7. Cover the eyes of bitterness with Son glasses!

Bitterness is usually seen through eyes that see an offense committed against us. We feel the heat of anger, rage and betrayal that burns inside.

> Esau said, "Isn't he rightly named Jacob? He has deceived me these two times: He took my birthright, and now he's taken my blessing!" Esau held a grudge against Jacob because of the blessing his father had given him. He said to himself, "The days of mourning for my father are near; then I will kill my brother Jacob."

Genesis 27:36, 41

When we put on Son glasses, God allows us to see things from his point of view (showing mercy, compassion and forgiveness). After twenty years apart, Esau saw his brother, ran to him and greeted him affectionately. The man, who at one time vowed to kill his brother over the bitterness of losing his birthright and blessing, was now changed letting time heal his bitter wounds. He forgave Jacob and God blessed him with ample wealth.

When we look past the emotion of bitterness (a cool look!)

and fix our eyes on the Son knowing he shows us mercy, compassion and forgiveness when we offend him, we can look at others with the same perspective.

> "Get rid of all bitterness, rage, and anger, brawling and slander along with every form of malice. Be kind and compassionate to one another, forgiving each other, just as Christ God forgave you"
>
> Ephesians 4:31–32

Fashion Basics: Three summer activities to inspire a cool look.
- Bask in the sunshine of God's love that burns eternally for you.
- Put on your bathing suit, go to the beach, and wade in the Living Water that washes sin away.
- While you watch the sunrise, let the rays of God's grace and mercy reflect the joy we have in Him!

Fall Fashion Forecast–Reality Dressing

Fall

The leaves are turning, the air is crisp, the winds of change are approaching. You feel the chill as the storms of life come knocking on the door. You reach into your closet and find the heavy coat of failure that weighs you down; the rain coat that once kept you dry is now drenched in adversity; the gloves that were so pliable are now placid and limiting your mobility, and the scarf that once warmed your heart is lost and can't be found.

Fall Fashion

While there are many patterns in life we fall into, here's one pattern you won't find on the fashion runway or pictured on the cover of any fashion magazine:

Failure

Adversity

Limitation

Loss (FALL)

To be honest, I was hesitant in presenting this fall pattern (maybe because I saw too much reality in it), but God impressed upon me to search to find his joy when I find myself unfashionably dressed for the bad and ugly realities I face in life.

Our design flaw is we have a sinful nature and our sinful

nature is usually our downfall. That's one reality we should recognize and accept. Sometimes all it takes is one popped button, one stuck zipper, a run in our pantyhose or not finding that "dang sweater" to begin a cycle of negative unproductive emotions and actions.

Fall Fashion Forecast

So you might ask what joy could possibly be found in failure, adversity, limitation and loss? To find the answer we have to look in our Fashion Guide.

> "Dear brothers and sisters, when troubles come your way consider it an opportunity for great joy. For you know that when your faith is tested, your endurance has a chance to grow."
>
> James 1:2–3, NLT

Joy is a feeling of happiness that comes from success, good fortune and a sense of well being, which is the opposite of how we feel when in the midst of fall. Our sinful nature falls prey to the feelings and emotions associated with a change in climate.

Reality

"And endurance develops strength of character and character strengthens our confident hope of salvation" (Romans 5:4, NLT).

In life we experience the good, the bad and the ugly.

- Ugly is trying to pair a polka dot shirt with a flower print skirt and failing to make it work

- Bad is finding a rip in your pantyhose that starts out small and runs through your good intentions, ruining a perfectly good plan

- Bad is wearing a jacket with the fabric stuck in the zipper; limited in movement—it just won't budge

- Ugly is a loss that doesn't know where it is and doesn't have any hope in finding its way

Dressing

"But don't just listen to God's word. You must do what it says" (James 1:22, NLT).

Dressing is a material used to cover an injury. When we fall we are emotionally injured. Emotional injuries like failure, adversity, limitation and loss need proper dressing (God) to recover so we can move on. The good news is, God equips us to dress in a fashion that's pleasing and brings glory to him in the fall.

Reality Dressing

"For we can rejoice, too, when we run into problems and trials, for we know that they help us develop endurance" (Romans 5:3, TLB).

If you look in my wardrobe you'll find fashions for the real world situations I find myself in. They are practical, down-to-earth garments built for durability and no-nonsense dressing. I call them my reality garments. I wear them when I need a reality check to get things straight in handling real life issues.

When our fall fashion forecast predicts stormy weather ahead, this is the right time to wear reality garments

Failure

Pairing a polka dot shirt with a flower print skirt is a fashion faux pas! It'll probably never work as a high-fashion look, no matter how we try. But recognizing that there will be times when we're being set up for failure is when polka dot perseverance and flower print wisdom can be an attractive look.

When the teachers of religious law and the leading priests challenged Jesus' authority, he recognized they were trying to set him up for failure. But in true Christ fashion, he persevered, using wisdom to foil their attempts.

Watching for their opportunity, the leaders sent spies pretending to be honest men. They tried to get Jesus to say something that could be reported to the Roman governor so he would arrest Jesus. "Teacher," they said, "we know that you speak and teach what is right and are not influenced by what others think. You teach the way of God truthfully. Now tell us—is it right for us to pay taxes to Caesar or not?" He saw through their trickery and said, "Show me a Roman coin. Whose picture and title are stamped on it?" "Caesar's," they replied. "Well then," he said, "give to Caesar what belongs to Caesar, and give to God what belongs to God." So they failed to trap him by what he said in front of the people. Instead, they were amazed by his answer, and they became silent."

Luke 20:20–26 (NLT)

The reality garment for failure is *perseverance*. This garment keeps trying, in spite of the difficulties, to get it right. It remains strong under pressure. James tells us to rejoice when we face difficulties because it adds strength to our character. Through reality dressing (applying God's Word) we find the joy of success in perseverance through failure.

Adversity

Pantyhose are delicate. They rip easily when coming in contact with rough objects. A rip may start out small, but if you don't get control, it runs all the way through to the end. While we can't control the adverse conditions we find ourselves falling into, we can control how we react to them. As a grown-up Joseph comforts his brothers, he tells them the most profound revelation. He said what they did to him was intended for his harm, but God intended it for his good. "You intended to harm me, but God intended it for good to accomplish what is now being done, the saving of many lives" (Genesis 50:20). Wow! That's the joy we find in adversity. Imagine if Joseph hadn't been cast away and sold as a slave—all of Egypt would have perished in the famine.

Endurance trains us to look for the joy in adversity. One thing we can count on is that God's love endures forever and whenever it is applied, it softens the heart of adversity.

The reality garment for adversity is *endurance*. "God blesses those who patiently endure testing and temptations. Afterward they will receive the crown of life that God has promised to those who love him" (James 1:12, NTL). Through reality dressing we search the scriptures and learn from those whose lives were blessed through patient endurance.

Fashion Tip #4

If you find a hole in your pantyhose apply clear nail polish around it to keep it from ripping any further. If you find yourself in an adverse situation, use Christ's nail polish: Scripture!

It's clear! Apply directly where adversity puts a hole in your good judgment so it won't run through your good intentions. Here's some "clear" nail polish for you to apply:

"We also pray that you will be strengthened with all his glorious power so you will have all the endurance and patience you need. May you be filled with joy, always thanking the Father. He has enabled you to share in the inheritance that belongs to his people, who live in the light."

Colossians 1:11-12 (NLT)

Limitation

Wearing a jacket with the fabric stuck in the zipper can be quite a challenge. Sometimes we hit a point where we can't go any farther in the direction we're going because we're stuck on our prideful ways. When we get stuck on the zipper of pride (having too high an opinion of our ability), we may fall into sin and fail to rely on God to free us from it.

The reality garment for limitation is humility—the quality of being humble (expressing a spirit of respect). When we wear humility there's no limit to what God can do in and through us. It opens the way to receiving God's favor. "…humbly accept the word of God that has been planted in your hearts, for it has the power to save your souls" (James 1:21, NTL). Through reality dressing we learn to practice prayer and ask God to remove the pattern of pride from the fabric of our being so we can move freely along the path of righteousness with Him leading the way!

"Pride leads to disgrace, but with humility comes wisdom" (Proverbs 11:2, NTL).

Loss

Loss is like frantically looking for your favorite sweater and remembering you lent it to your best friend who just recently moved to another state!

I included loss in this fall pattern because it is a reality of life. *Hope* is the reality garment for loss.

Reality dressing *h*angs *o*n *p*romises *e*ternally. Hope is boundless in its comfort ability. Jesus promised to never leave us. He gave us the Holy Spirit to comfort us. Not just for special occasions—always! Through reality dressing we learn that hope works when we put it on and wear it! If you're having trouble finding hope in the dark places of your life, turn on his Light! "And this hope will not lead to disappointment. For we know how dearly God loves us because he has given us the Holy Spirit to fill our hearts with his love" (Romans 5:5, NLT).

In the process of developing my passion for God's fashion, I'm learning to believe in God's promises, even when they haven't materialized. While we don't have the ability to forecast the "whether" conditions (whether we'll experience them or not), we can find joy through perseverance, endurance, humility and hope in reality dressing to create a new fall pattern—face it, accept it, learn from it and live through it—and see God's promises materialize, just as he intended! "Now all glory to God, who is able to keep you from falling away and will bring you with great joy into his glorious presence without a single fault" (Jude 1:24, NLT).

"I came that they may have and enjoy life, and have it in abundance (to the full, till it overflows)" (John 10:10, TAB).

The Wardrobe

"Your baptism in Christ was not just washing you up for a fresh start. It also involved dressing you in an adult faith wardrobe—Christ's life, the fulfillment of God's original promise."

Galatians 3:27, MSG

Up to this point we have learned about The Passion and seen some of The Fashion. Before we get into The Shopping, let's focus on The Wardrobe.

Our wardrobe is made up of many fashions we wear daily. It changes as we change in size, style and vocation. It projects our sense of style and individual personality.

What to Wear

A well-functioning wardrobe consists of fashions that fit well, look good on us, and make us feel good when we wear them. It adapts to many occasions. You can tell your wardrobe isn't working for you anymore if every time you look in your closet (full of fashions) and find you have nothing to wear. In this case, you may need a new wardrobe!

It's important to try fashions on before you buy them. I don't have enough fingers to count the number of times I've gone shopping and bought things I liked without trying them on first, only to discover they don't fit me or don't integrate well into my current wardrobe. Instead of returning them, I put them in my closet hoping that "someday" I'd grow (or shrink) into them, or eventually find something that coordinates.

I think our wardrobe should be built with purpose. If you

Fashion...Forward
Did you know that our Fashion Guide tells about future fashion trends? Read The Revelation to know the truth!

---

don't have a purpose for particular fashions (just liking them doesn't count!), they shouldn't be part of your wardrobe. They serve no other purpose than to take up space in the closet, and continual accumulation leads to clutter and chaos.

A Purposeful Wardrobe

Do you know the Designer has a purpose for us? He allows us to try on His fashions to help us discover our purpose until we feel confident wearing them.

"So if you're serious about living this new resurrection life with Christ, act like it. Pursue the things over which Christ presides" (Colossians 3:1, MSG)

A purposeful wardrobe must function well to suit our needs. It should project our individual style, personality and adapt to our changing needs.

A purposeful wardrobe must purge the old (way of doing) to make room for the new (life in Christ*)*. "Your old life is dead. Your new life, which is your real life—even though invisible to spectators—is with Christ in God. He is your life" (Colossians 3:3, MSG).

To determine if your spiritual and physical wardrobe is purposed well, you need to go to the closet.

Here are five closet rules for a purposeful wardrobe:

Examine

Decide

Empty

Inventory

Organize

Examine your closet and study its contents.

Can you remember the last time you took time to look in your closet to see what's there? By nature we are creatures of habit. Do you find that when you get up in the morning each day, you reach into a dark closet and pull out the same old attitudes and emotions you had on the day before? The danger in reaching into a dark closet is that you can't see what you've put on until halfway through the day when the busyness of life has taken its toll on you!

Decide what should and shouldn't be stored.

Sort through things you no longer wear, don't fit you anymore, or need mending. Do you have things that not longer fit you like anger, bitterness or stress? Are your shelves packed with impatience and intolerance? Do you have shoes "too big to fill"?

Empty the entire contents.

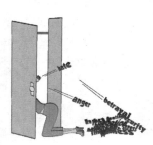

The closet is the container of our wardrobe and should be periodically cleared out and reorganized to house our fashions efficiently and effectively.

Our closet (the mind) contains our motives, attitudes and emotions. Life stresses and time pressures create a lifestyle of thoughts and actions we put on to cope with life issues. While we deal with things "the way we've always done it," it may not be using good fashion sense (the right way to handle the situation). I find in times of frustration and impatience, I'd speak negatively or react in the moment. It became an instinctive reaction that usually brought about negative consequences, like guilt and hurt feelings.

When our closet becomes full and disorganized, we can't think clearly or objectively. It leaves room for the enemy's attacks because he's at work on us when things are chaotic and we're caught off guard. God wants us to think clearly so we can understand His direction for us, and that's hard to do when our closet is cluttered and diverted from Him.

The best way I've found to clear my closet is to do some vacuuming. I do a brain dump on paper. When thoughts are written down, they no longer have to be retained, so the mind releases them. Then I pray. I confess to God all of the negative thoughts, emotions and attitudes that have been allowed to take hold in my mind. I ask God to purge them from my closet to make room for the new fashions He desires me to wear.

Hangers

Have you ever tried to pull something out of the closet and find that it's caught on something? The more you pull, the more tangled it becomes!

Hangers serve one purpose, to hold fashions we put in the closet, but different kinds of hangers are used to hang specific types of fashions. What types of hangers do you have in your closet?

Plastic

Plastic hangers come in many colors and are designed to hold lightweight fashions. If you put too much weight on them, they buckle and eventually break. When we're prideful or hang our security on unrealistic expectations, they may buckle under the disappointment we feel and break our trust.

Wire

Wire hangers are strong, but if you let fashions hang on them too long, they crease or wrinkle fashions and clothes have to be ironed out before you can wear them again. When we let unresolved anger or unforgiveness hang too long on our peace, it will need to be ironed out before peace can be worn comfortably.

Wood

Wood hangers cost more but are well worth the investment because they can hold a lot of weight; they won't bend or break under pressure or cause creases or wrinkle your fashions. "The LORD is good, a strength and stronghold in the day of trouble; He knows [recognizes, has knowledge of, and understands] those who take refuge and trust in Him" (Nahum 1:7, TAB).

Hooks

You can find some hangers equipped with hooks to hold fashion accessories and sometimes the hooks get caught on fashions hanging too close to them.

If we find we get caught on the hooks (situations) that snag us into acting ugly, we need to take time to unhook or untangle ourselves from the situation. Knowing Satan does things to hook us into acting ugly, we must always be mindful to keep from getting caught up in his attempts to snag us away from God. "Let us throw off everything that hinders and the sin that so easily entangles, and let us run with perseverance the race marked out for us" (Hebrews 12:1).

Doctor's visits are one situation that hooks my anger and catches me acting ugly. When I get there I'm on time and expect to be seen in a timely fashion, so I can tend to the other ten things on my "to do" list. But when I arrive, I always have to wait, sometimes as long as an hour. The longer I sit, the madder I get because I feel my time is being wasted just sitting and waiting.

I think God sometimes allows situations to reoccur to help us learn the right way to act and deal with them. Knowing I always have to wait makes me more impatient and angry, and that's exactly the reaction Satan wants from me.

It wasn't until I decided to make productive use of my waiting time that I realized I needed an attitude adjustment. When I began to look at the time I spent waiting as a "joy break," I began to relax and come up with ways to entertain myself with the much needed downtime I desired. By the time the nurse would call me in to see the doctor I'd given thanks to God for giving me time to "be still and know" and truly enjoy my joy break!

Fashion Tip #5

When you feel Satan trying to hook you into acting ugly, be determined to make an attitude adjustment. Say "Get behind me Satan. You can't block my Son light and you don't have the power to steal my joy."

"Therefore submit to God. Resist the devil and he will flee from you."

James 4:7 (NKJV)

Hanger Do's and Don'ts

Do hang your fashions facing in one direction to create a unified-look. When everything is facing the right way, you can easily see how to make them work together. "And we know that God causes all things to work together for good to those who love God, to those who are called according to His purpose" (Romans 8:28, NASB).

Don't hang too many fashions on one hanger. The added weight may cause them to fall and need to be picked up off of the floor.

If we let Satan throw too many temptations on our joy we may find it giving in to the pressure and fall into sin. Remembering Satan's goal is to kill, steal and destroy; "Be sober! Be on alert! Your adversary the devil is prowling around like a roaring lion, looking for anyone he can devour" (1 Peter 5:8, HCSB), reminds us to free ourselves from the hooks designed to catch us by looking for a way out to keep us from giving into it. "But remember that the temptations that come into your life are no different from what others experience. And God is faithful. He will keep that temptation from becoming so strong that you can't stand up against it. When you are tempted, he will show you a way out so that you will not give in to it" (1 Corinthians 10:13, NLT).

Do invest in well-made, sturdy hangers to keep your fashions looking good and ready to wear without special treatment.

Don't hang your faith on plastic or wire hangers. If you have a wooden hanger (trust in God), consider hanging your faith on it. I hang my faith on trust in God because He is strong and unbreakable. I trust that my faith will hang free without hooks to get snagged or caught on. I hang my faith without worry and am assured that there won't be any creases or wrinkles found. Trust in God never fails to hold my faith in a presentable manner for me to put on and wear at all times for Him!

My emotions and attitudes change as often (or more) than I

Fashion Tip #6

When hanging your fashions in a clean, organized, inspired closet, consider the value of the hangers you choose to put them on. They may look good but if they're not purposed to hold the things you put on them, what value can be found in them?

do, but one thing remains the same—God. He is faithful and always ready and willing to hold me up, even when I'm heavy with faults and weaknesses.

Fashion Tip #7

Invest in sturdy, well-made hangers. You don't want to hang your hope on flimsy truth or your trust on something that breaks too easily!

Now that you have a clean, good looking, empty closet, let me take this opportunity to bring in some inspiration. What if I told you your physical closet can be a place for you to get spiritual inspiration to wear throughout the day. Would you believe me? You would've probably said "no" before reading this book, but now that you've gotten to know me a little better, I'll bet you believe me (smile).

Inspiration in Your Closet

Have you ever had "one of those days"? You know, when you hit the snooze button for the last time, open your eyes and realize you're not in Kansas anymore?

You jump out of bed grumbling because you're going to be late for work, head for the bathroom with one eye open. Then to the closet to find something to wear because you forgot to lay out your clothes the night before. You're mad at yourself; frustrated you have to rush, and stressed just thinking about all the things you have to do for the day. Before you've even had a chance to thank God for letting you live to see another day, Satan is already on your heels. You're angry, frustrated, stressed and it's only 7:00 a.m.!

When you think about it, the closet is one of the first places we go to prepare ourselves for the day. It has the potential to set the tone for how we're going to feel throughout the entire day. While anger, frustration and stress is not the desired inspiration, we feel that way sometimes and it's hard to shake those emotions without something positive to redirect our focus.

People use different methods for inspiration. Some read affirmations on the bathroom mirror while brushing their teeth in the morning. Some make "to do" lists and refer to them often to refresh their memory for what needs to be accomplished for the day. I feel Monday mornings can sometimes be particularly inspiration-challenged. It's usually then we realize this is the first day of a long work week ahead! How do we use our real-life closet to set the tone for starting the day off right?

Can you picture yourself getting up in the morning looking in your closet and finding joy and peace hanging there for you to put on? Would it motivate you to wear joy and peace for the day (even if it's Monday morning)? I get inspired just thinking about it! I'll bet by now I've peaked your curiosity. Do you want to know how I plan to put inspiration into both of your closets? Well I'll tell you (you knew I would). It's done with "I-tags."

When my boys were small we bought them a brand of clothing called Garanimals. Each article had a tag of an animal attached to help the child identify coordinating tops and bottoms by simply matching the tags. While I'm not asking you to put animal tags on your clothes, I like the idea of putting tags on my hangers, so every time I pull out something, I have something to look at and think about. I-tags serve two purposes. First, they are visible inspiration. When we see things, we focus our mind on them and allow the mind to process them. Second, they offer spiritual inspiration for "I statements" like "I will wear joy and peace throughout the day." "You will live in joy and peace" (Isaiah 55:12, NLT).

"I statements" are purposed and willful to prepare you to not only "put on" but also to "wear" God's Fashions for the day.

Simple right? You already have a clean closet. You've got sturdy, well-made hangers, now let's get busy adding some inspiration for our fashions to hang on!

I-tag Directions:

1. Use one word for each I-tag. The word can be glued, painted

> Fashion Tip #8
> The best place to find a variety of words for your I-tags is in the concordance of our Fashion Guide. Also, use different variations of a word to create different I-tag inspirations like faith, faithful and faithfulness.

or written on in any style to grab your attention. If you have two hanging racks that occupy the same space for tops and bottoms, make two sets of the same words to have many inspirations (different combinations) throughout the days, weeks and months to come! Cardstock paper is a great heavyweight paper to use. If you want to make your I-tags last longer and be sturdier, laminate them. If you are the adventurous type, use different colored paper for your I-tags. Use either light gray, tan or white to give a uniform look to your closet.

2. Pick a shape to use as a template and cut out several from the cardstock in different sizes like pictured above. Craft

stores have pre-cut shapes to buy if you want to save time and effort.

3. Make a hole with a hole-punch and thread ribbon or wire through the hole and tie a knot. Tie a bow at the top and put on your hanger. Try to put your I-Tag close to the top of the hanger and keep them no more than about two inches in diameter to keep them from getting tangled in the clothes.

Creative Uses for Your I-tags
Subject-Motivated Inspiration

If you normally lay out your clothes at night, here's a great fifteen-minute inspiration-starter for you.

1. Write down the I-tag words found on your hangers.
2. Look in your Fashion Guide to find scripture relating to your I-tags and write them down.
3. As you pray about what you've read, ask God to reveal a personal meaning, purpose and way to apply the truth of your inspirations.
4. Take five minutes to write down an "I statement" for each word.
5. Not only will you grow from the knowledge gained by spending time studying and meditating on the Word, you will have a foundation for inspired thinking!
6. As you plan things to get done for the day, recall your "I statements" and write them down on your "to do" list. This will keep your mind focused on your inspiration and keep motivating you throughout the day.

Share Your Inspiration

Fashion Tip #9

If you have children, help them create inspiration in their closet! Work with them to create their own I-tags. Use their children's Fashion Guide to find I-tag words. It will have age-appropriate words children identify with. Use cookie cutters as templates. Children can trace around them easily, and they'll love making the fun shapes. Let them decorate the I-tags and write down one word on each. Use a hole punch and thread ribbon through. Help them put the I-tags on their hangers. Now they also have a closet full of inspiration! Before your children leave for school, ask them to recall their inspiration word(s). Help them come up with an "I" statement like "I will wear joy in my heart today"; and perhaps think of ways to help them demonstrate their "I" statement in school. This is a great way for us to put God on our children and have them wear Him throughout the day.

As parents, there's great joy in knowing we're instrumental in developing a passion (passing it on) for God in our children. A good way is to give them inspiration—in Godly fashion!

"And now a word to you parents. Don't keep on scolding and nagging your children, making them angry and resentful. Rather bring them up with the loving discipline the Lord himself approves, with suggestions and godly advice."

Ephesians 6:4 (TKB)

If you share a closet like I do, it can be a place for you and your spouse to have shared inspiration! While making my I-tags, my husband looked at them and asked me what they were. As I began to tell him and share how I was using them, he decided he liked them too and wanted me to make some for his hangers! We decided to meet in the closet to talk about the inspirations we find there. This has become an inspiring way for us to communicate and share with each other.

Inspired Walking

1. Here's a great idea to get you walking in style.

2. Fill a small organza bag with lavender, mint or lemon herbs. I use herbs from tea bags. I simply snip the top of the bag and pour the herbs into the organza bag.

3. Slip an I-Tag on the ribbon of the bag and close.

4. Insert your sachet into your shoes (deodorizing).

Now when you go to your closet to put on your shoes, you have inspiration for your walk with God!

Fashion Tip #10: Walk in Faith
You can always do like Dorothy in the Wizard of Oz to get inspired. Close your eyes. Visualize your I-Tag word. Click your heels three times and say, "There's no place I'd rather be than in the presence of God." Now open your eyes. Viola!

Be inspired knowing you are in the presence of God. He will never leave you or forsake you when you abide in him. That's a promise! Now open the door and be on your way inspired to walk with God.

"For shoes, put on the peace that comes from the Good News, so that you will be fully prepared."

Ephesians 6:15 (NLT)

Give an Inspiring Gift

Buy three decorative hangers. Make four I-tags (three for the hangers and one for a shoe sachet). On the back of each, write down the book name, chapter number and verse from your Fashion Guide that relates to the I-tag word.

On the gift card, write down the purpose and use for your gift. You could write something like "As you hang your fashions on these special hangers, find inspiration in the words to help you wear the truth of God's love every day."

These are just a few creative ways to inspire you to think about God and live knowing you are divinely fashioned in His mercy. He gives new mercy every day. It's a gift that is undeserved, can't be bought or earned, and receiving it isn't dependent on anything we've done—good or bad. We need to be inspired in order to live the kind of life God has designed for us.

The closet is just one place we can go for inspiration and because we go there every day, we have reminders to put God on, wear his fashions and walk with him every day in **G*S.T.Y.L.E.!**

1. Inventory Your Wardrobe

    When I inventory my attitudes, emotions and feelings, I try to get rid of things that no longer fit me like unforgiveness, sadness, unrealistic expectations and trying to change people. I discard things that don't look good on me anymore like gossip, envy and insecurity. I also separate the things that need mending like hurt feelings, anxiety and stress.

    What I'm left with are some fashions that still fit me like kindness, compassion and a giving heart; fashions that look good on me like faithfulness, caring and goodness of spirit; fashions that make me feel good when I wear them like joy, peace, love and thankfulness.

    Take time to inventory your wardrobe. Examine what you have and what you need to acquire. Be determined to eliminate what no longer fits, doesn't look good or makes you feel insecure when you wear them. Take the things that need mending to God. He cares for you and desires for you to wear His fashions.

2. Organize to Create Balance and Order
    As you look at your clean closet, carefully consider what will be put back. We need to organize for balance and order. Consider adding adjustable, multi-level rods to double the space. Consider your thoughts. Allowing negative thoughts

to take up residence makes us negative-minded (remember that as a man thinks, so shall he become). Conversely, positive thinking yields positive results.

Fashion Tip #11
It's always good to place a laundry basket (confession) in your closet to put dirty things (sin) in one place (at the foot of the cross) to be washed (by Jesus) weekly.

Things should be ordered for accessibility, so organize to access the fashions you wear most often in plain view and within easy reach. Don't let clutter like anger and impatience obstruct your view. Designate space for storage and group like-items together.

Three Ways to Jazz Up Your Physical Closet

Try adding color to the walls. Most people don't bother painting the closet, but adding color brings new life to a neutral closet!

Add coat hooks and shelves to maximize the vertical space. Most times, our eye is drawn to the space we see right in front of us, but utilizing vertical space draws our eye up to allow us to see things with a different perspective!

Use attractive storage containers. Storing things in containers keeps clutter under control. Group like-items together, label and store. I have tried, with minimal success, to memorize scripture without labeling them first. I find I memorize and recall scripture better when I have a label to apply them to like "insecurity" or "worry." Memorize scripture to store in your mind to recall when applicable. I often use the concordance of our Fashion Guide to find multiple scriptures for each label. On days when

I feel insecure about something, I have my like-items (related scriptures) labeled and stored, which make me feel more secure. You can always recall one favorite, but having more adds reinforcement to put you back on track! Having my security packed in an attractive container (trust in God) is more appealing to me than when I pack it in my own brown box!

Once you've established balance and order, and inventoried your wardrobe, you're ready put back only the things appropriate for you to wear efficiently and effectively. With purpose!

Exclusive Collection

"So, chosen by God for this new life of love, dress in the wardrobe God picked out for you: compassion, kindness, humility, quiet strength, discipline" (Colossians 3:12, MSG).

"Must-Have" Fashions

"Must-have" fashions are the core (foundation) fashions that anchor your wardrobe. They provide timeless style and wear. Once you've established a set of core fashions, you can begin searching for the 'stand out' fashions that really make your wardrobe work for you.

If after evaluating your wardrobe, you find it's lacking some of the core fashions listed below, study your Fashion Guide for timely wisdom and fashion advice.

> The fundamental fact of existence is that this trust in
> God, this faith, is the firm foundation under everything
> that makes life worth living. It's our handle on what we
> can't see.
>
> (Hebrews 11:1, MSG)

By faith, we see the world called into existence by God's word, what we see created by what we don't see.

(Hebrews 11:3, MSG)

It's impossible to please God apart from faith. And why? Because anyone who wants to approach God must believe both that he exists and that he cares enough to respond to those who seek him.

Hebrews 11:6, MSG

Fashion Tip #12
Freshen up your wardrobe by adding something new. Try on something you've never worn before like teaching, mentoring or leading a Bible study. If it fits you well, incorporate it into your wardrobe. It will give a fresh new look to what you already have!

Acquire fashions that "stand-out"

These fashions compliment or coordinate with the core fashions. They project your individual style. Though some are classically styled, they offer modern, up-to-date styling and always look good when worn properly. Here's a few of the stand-out fashions you'll probably be wearing in the near future.

"So, chosen by God for this new life of love, dress in the wardrobe God picked out for you:

- compassion

- kindness

- humility

- quiet strength

- discipline

- be even-tempered

- content with second place

- quick to forgive an offense.

- Forgive as quickly and completely as the Master forgave you."(Colossians 3:12–13)

"And regardless of what else you put on, wear love. It's your basic, all-purpose garment. Never be without it" (Colossians 3:14, MSG).

A to Z Accessorizing

Here are some great accessories to add some **G*S.T.Y.L.E.** passion to your fashions.

A–Appreciate all you have, count your many blessings. Name them one by one.

B–Believe!

C–Celebrate your life in Christ and shout for joy.

D–Develop your passion for God.

E–Every day try to put on an "Attitude of Gratitude."

F–Focus on God.

G–Grace is a gift from God; go and tell the Good News.

H–Humbly walk in the footsteps of Christ.

I–Ignite your passion; read your Fashion Guide.

J–Joyfully receive the Holy Spirit.

K–Keep balance and order to prevent chaos.

L–Love others as God loves you.

M–Mercy is made new every day!

N–Note some things God has given you by writing him a love letter.

O–Open your mind to the Word of God.

P–Praise God.

Q–Quietly surrender.

R–Renew, refresh and rejuvenate your passion for God.

S–Savor the moment with thankful prayer.

T–Trust the fashion sense God gave you.

U–Use the gifts God has given to you.

V–Volunteer your time and talents to others.

W–Walk in newness of life in Christ.

X–X-press yourself with rejoicing.

Y–Yellow is bright and warm just like the Son.

Z–Zealously pursue your passion for God's Fashion.

The Runway Collection

The Runway Collection is what the fashion industry uses to forecast the "in" fashions for the season. "In" fashions are centered on a theme, style or color combination that's usually not the norm.

Seasonal fashions are not meant to be integrated into your wardrobe. They are worn with core fashions and when the season is over, they are rarely worn again. Some are designed to fit an occasion like Easter, Christmas or a wedding.

When my sister and I were little, my mom dressed us (usually the same) in Easter outfits. Those white patent-leather shoes and fluffy dresses usually meant spring was just around the corner.

A wedding dress is appropriate for a bride to wear at her wedding, but not appropriate for grocery shopping. Besides the obvious stares you'd receive as you make your way down the vegetable aisle, that long dress could get caught up in the wheels of the shopping cart!

When dressing appropriately for the season of life you're in, wear the "in" fashions for the season.

If you are in a season of planting, water your mind with the Word and get plenty of Son shine because your soul is fertile (prepared) to make the seed of knowledge and truth grow.

I have a friend who is in a season of mourning; "Blessed are those who mourn, for they will be comforted" (Matthew 5:4). Her husband went to be with the LORD a couple of years ago. In her season of grief, sadness, loneliness and depression, she has learned to wear comfort and hope for the future because the Son shines bright in her. He has lovingly adorned her in the grace and joy that comes in the morning; "…weeping may remain for a night, but rejoicing comes in the morning" (Psalm 30:5).

Discovering which season we're in requires examination of our circumstances, how we react to them, and the attitudes and emotions we carry that drive our actions. Scripture reminds us we will go through different seasons in our life.

"To everything there is a Season." It also reminds us that there is a reason (a purpose) for experiencing seasons. "A time for every purpose under Heaven." Because seasons change, we are assured we will go through them for a time so we need to create outfits for different seasons.

The Wisdom of Solomon in Ecclesiastes details the seasons and studying them helps us understand and accept them as a part of life.

I think you'll find the reason for the season (either after you've gone through it, or in the midst) when you continually seek God for the answers. He will help you put on the right outfit for the season.

Blessings in Hand-Me-Downs

A few years ago I went through a season of panic attacks. I wasn't dressed appropriately for the season I was in. I wore fear, worry, anxiety and stress. My spirit was exposed to the elements (Satan's attacks) that weakened my immunity to fight off the sleepless nights, exhaustion and depression. My sister, Anita, went through the same season a couple of years before and handed down her seasonal fashions to me. She shared her wisdom on how to deal with and conquer the panic attacks, and she pointed me to books written by others who had been through the same season. I read in our Fashion Guide about Solomon's season of darkness and could identify with his state of mind. My sister blessed me through her hand-me-downs, and enabled me to dress appropriately through the season.

A few months ago, while writing this book, my son, Andre' (now twenty-one) shared with me that he too was in that fearful season. You'd think someone so young wouldn't be in this season, but I find anytime God's children are moving closer to Him, the cold and flu season (Satan's attacks) comes. I was able to hand down to him the same blessings I received from my sister, and now he has made it through. Hopefully he will be blessed to pass on (the passion), his hand-me-downs to someone else.

God's seasonal fashions are powerful. They provide protection from the elements to give us time to get through. We are blessed whenever we willingly receive the protection He offers us.

I think hand-me-downs offer a special blessing when "birds of a feather flock together." From time to time my girlfriends and I have "911 Lemonade" nights. When one of us is being challenged by the lemons of life, we get together to pray for and comfort each other by offering timely advice and care. Our 911 Lemonade nights came out of a ladies' weekend getaway I aptly themed "When life throws you lemons, make lemonade!" We learned ways to use the lemons of life to make us grow (that's another book!). Hand-me-downs offer something you won't find in new seasonal fashions. They have the wisdom from others who've worn them as designed. We flock together for those who are unable to dress themselves appropriately for the season, to pass on the blessings and help them make it through.

Fashion Tip #13
If you find that you're not dressed appropriately for the season you're in right now and someone hasn't handed down their seasonal fashions to you, go to the "Salvation Army" (Christ) or the "Goodwill" (still Christ) to find the appropriate clothing.

There's no shame in hand-me-downs, only blessings, because hand-me-downs come with comfort built in. They have already been broken in and washed for you. They come with assurance that wearing them will keep you appropriately dressed for as long as you need.

Jesus handed down His Spirit through tongues of fire on high for all those present at Pentecost and to us today. From what they received, they freely gave to others.

The circle of giving, and receiving and blessings is endless.

Giving is a spiritual gift and those who receive it with the right heart are blessed.

The next time you are tempted to pack up your seasonal fashions or throw them away, look for someone to give them to. There may be a family member, friend or co-worker who isn't dressed for the season they are in. Let them be blessed by receiving what you have to give and you'll be blessed by giving what you've already worn. There are many blessings in hand-me-downs!

Now you have the makings of a wardrobe with purpose. With careful examination and determination, you'll have a new

wardrobe custom-made with a purpose and inspiration to motivate you to clothe yourself wonderfully in Christ.

"Now you're dressed in a new wardrobe. Every item of your
new way of life is custom-made by the Creator, with his label on
it. All the old fashions are now obsolete" (Colossians 3:10, MSG).

The Shopping

Shopping: to visit shops for the purpose of looking over and acquiring goods
—Shopper

To shop (search Him on purpose) is a good thing. To have a shopping experience is a great thing! Searching Him on purpose is a willful act of seeking God. The experience comes from searching Him on purpose continually! That's what the passion of "The Shopping" is all about.

Have you seen the bumper sticker that says "Born to Shop"? I think they had me in mind when they created it! If you weren't born to shop, you can always be "reborn" to experience shopping. Simply close your eyes, open your heart, and ask God to come into your life.

My passion for fashion is fueled by The Shopping, which is about seeking and finding. "You will seek Me and find Me when you search for Me with all your heart" (Jeremiah 29:13, NASB)

Sometimes you find exactly what you are looking for, and sometimes you find great joy in the unexpected; the things you weren't looking for but found because you were seeking. "But seek first his kingdom and his righteousness and all these things will be given to you as well" (Mathew 6:33).

Savvy shoppers of God's fashions shop for the purpose of looking for and acquiring God's goods. They can't be bought or sold; only given and received. God's goods are priceless but affordable to all who are willing to look for them and pay by giving thanks.

And speaking of God's goods, be assured that when you shop, you'll find racks of his goods in abundance. Savvy shoppers also know the key to successful shopping—commit. "Commit your activities to the LORD and your plans will be achieved" (Proverbs 16:3, HCSB).

As we prepare for The Shopping, let me give you some power tools to help make your shopping experience fun, exciting, purposeful and meaningful. You'll want to make plans for your next shopping trip!

Create a shopping list:

1. **Assess your clothing needs**

   After examining your wardrobe, you probably have a good idea of your clothing needs. Assess what you have and what you need to acquire. Look over the "must-haves" and "stand-out" fashions.

   "Until now you have not asked for anything in my name. Ask and you will receive, and your joy will be complete" (John 16:24, HCSB).

   Do you need more mix-n-match fashions like forgiveness and compassion to coordinate with all your mercies? Do you have enough suits for year-round comfort and wear? "Put on the full armor of God so that you can stand against the tactics of the Devil" (Ephesians 6:11, HCSB). Do you need more patterns of love to make your joy complete?

   This year I've determined I need more self-control to stand up against all my temptations. Do your homework. Take inventory of your clothing needs so you can shop with confidence.

   "In all your ways acknowledge him, and he will make your paths straight" (Proverbs 3:6).

   List what is needed to fill in your basic wardrobe.

   As you rid your closet of things that no longer fit, need mending, and don't look good on you anymore, you probably have space for new fashions to freshen up your wardrobe.

Take time to make a list of things you need to shop for. Making a list ensures you don't forget what's needed and provides purpose for shopping.

If you're not sure of what all you need, look through your Fashion Guide and jot down things you'd like to have. Ask a trusted friend to help you develop your list. Friends can see what you lack and can advise you based on what they think your needs are.

Organize your list into categories.

"God has given gifts to each of you from his great variety of spiritual gifts. Manage them well so that God's generosity can flow through you" (1 Peter 4:10, NLT).

Categorizing makes it easier to locate specialty stores that carry certain brands of fashions you'll be looking for.

You can put strength, fearlessness, and encouragement under courage to keep it standing strong—Joshua 1:9

Never ending mercies and faithfulness are a category of love—Lamentations 3:22–23

You can also define categories by how you'll use them, for example, "to benefit others." You might list kindness, gentleness, teaching and forgiving. "I statements" make great categories because they have use and fashion built in. "I will wear peace and joy in my heart today." Whichever way you decide, make your list have meaning so you can easily plan where, when and how you'll be shopping.

2. Planning

"Careful planning puts you ahead in the long run; hurry and scurry puts you further behind" (Proverbs 21:5, msg). Examine your schedule and devote time for shopping.

Hast makes waste. When pressed for time, don't plan to shop in stores that carry a wide variety of fashions because you won't have enough time to shop for everything on your list. Plan to "power shop" in specialty stores that carry fashions in one category on your list. Stores like James are power packed with fashions for wisdom.

"But the wisdom that comes from heaven is first of all pure and full of quiet gentleness. Then it is peace loving and continuous. It allows discussion and is willing to yield to others' it is full of mercy and good deeds. It is whole hearted and straight forward and sincere" (James 3:17 TLB).

When you make time for shopping, plan to go to different stores to see many of the same fashions displayed in different ways. Love is found in many places. In some it's displayed in affection and in others it's shown in reverence.

Fashion Tip #14.

Use a personal shopper. If you feel overwhelmed shopping in large stores like Proverbs, consider using a personal shopper (God). Your personal shopper accompanies you throughout the store. He will advise you and pull together some appropriate fashions for you to try on; ones you might not have chosen for yourself, never considered wearing, or missed seeing.

"The Lord says "I will guide you along the best pathway for your life. I will advise you and watch over you."

Psalm 32:8 (NLT)

Our Fashion Guide has the names and locations of sixty-six places to shop. Use the directory; the concordance to find addresses (Scripture) of the stores that carry fashions on your list so you'll know exactly where to look.

If you plan to do some gift shopping, 1 Corinthians is one place you'll want to frequent. Look on 12th St.; there you'll find some spiritual gifts. If you'll plan to shop in bulk to find enough prayers for patience, you'll want to go to Psalms. You'll find it between Job and Proverbs. It carries many prayers to sustain you.

"Why am I praying like this? Because I know you will answer me, O God! Yes listen as I pray. Show me your strong love in wonderful ways, O Savior of all those seeking your help against their foes" (Psalm 17:6–7, TLB).

If you fail to take time to think about where you'll shop, you may find yourself in a place of confusion. "In thee, O Lord, do I put my trust; let me never be put to confusion." (Psalm 71:1, KJV)

I'm one of those people who has a terrible sense of direction. When I'm lost, I'm confused and anxious to the point of crying. Knowing the direction I'm going in and how to get there keeps me calm and able to find my way.

Fashion Tip #15
Write the addresses (Scripture) of stores you'll frequent and record them in your planner to refer to when planning your next shopping trip. You can also use it to show others some of the best places to shop!

Shopping Tips

Shop with a budget in mind. Take time to search Him on purpose. Set aside a clothing allowance to make sure you get all you need to be adequately clothed.

Do some window-shopping to get an idea of what's in the various stores. Open your Fashion Guide and read the first chapter in each store. This will provide a glimpse of the exciting things you'll find when you do your shopping there.

Include power shopping to find places to learn about the power of the Holy Spirit. Shopping in Acts 2 is where you find the awesome power of the tongues of fire; everyone there was touched by the Holy Spirit. They heard the declarations of the wonders of God in their native tongue, even though spoken in languages different from their own (Acts 2:11)!

If you're a music lover you must shop in Psalms. It has 150 "all occasion" musical selections to soothe the soul. Look for praise music, love songs, melodies, moody blues, jazz and instrumentals (harps, trumpet sounds, etc.), and sing for joy.

For future fashion trends, you have to check out Revelation. There you'll find a variety of trendy styles. You'll also be blessed by shopping there (Revelation 1:3). It is the only store that promises a blessing to those who hear it and take to heart what is written in it.

I feel confident now that you have everything you need for our shopping trip. Now, get some rest and meet me bright and early. Don't forget your directions (I don't want you to get lost!), and your shopping list!

"All Aboard!"

I'm glad you could join me on the Almighty Express! I trust you didn't have trouble finding track seven using the directions I gave you and I hope you remembered to bring your Master's Card. The conductor will be around shortly to check our tickets, so find a seat and get comfortable. Today we'll shop at one of my favorite fashion boutiques. It has fashions and accessories hand-picked by the Designer. While we ride, feel free to browse our Fashion Guide in the pocket on the back of the seat in front of you to view some of the fashions we'll be seeing today.

"All Aboard! Last Call!" I'm so excited.

I especially like boutique shopping because they have things you won't find in most large retail stores. Most often you find fashions and accessories that reflect the unique style of the owner. My favorite color is purple and one time I stopped by a shop in Washington D.C. called "Purple Passion." Everything in there was some shade of purple, and of course I had to go in and check it out! The shop owner came over and greeted me. She shared some stories with me about her passion for purple. Since I shared her passion, I found many purple things to take home with me that day!

Some boutiques carry such exclusive fashions that people travel many miles just to own them. I know that living in the Internet age, we can easily acquire exclusives by a simple click of the mouse, but it just isn't the same as being there. That's the passion of shopping!

Well, we're almost there! Can you feel the excitement in the air? When I first came here, I couldn't wait for the train to stop. I had read all about the fashions in our Fashion Guide and I couldn't wait to see them for myself. My sister, Anita, was sitting right beside me and I think she was as excited as I was!

Recently I have been working closely with the Designer and He wanted me to share with you my passion for His fashions. I was so taken by my experience there that I decided to be a spokesperson, a fashion consultant to help lead others to shop there.

Let me tell you about the first time I came here. This exclusive boutique was nothing like other shops I'd seen before. There was a narrow doorway and no windows on the front, so I couldn't see what was inside until I opened the door. When I walked in I found it was much larger on the inside than it appeared from the front. There were large marble columns surrounding the front desk with a beautifully designed book for the attendant to write my name in. The attendant greeted me warmly and handed me a shopping bag.

She told me how the boutique was wonderfully designed in sections, each with aisle numbers containing numbered racks and shelves. She also took time to tell me some things about the Designer so I could appreciate the quality and value in His fashions.

- He is the Creator and originator of fashion.

- He's been in the business since the beginning of time.

- His fashions are well known around the world, sought after by many and worn by famous people.

- His fashions have been worn by kings and are easily recognizable by His designer label.

- His fashions never go out of style and they look better the more you wear them.

- His fashions are exclusive because they are manufactured in one place.

- Each piece comes with His personal Care label.

- His signature colors are royal purple, blood red and snow white.

After finding all of this out, I couldn't wait to go shopping! As I strolled down the Job section in aisle 14, I found on rack

10 clothing made of honor and majesty beautifully adorned with glory and splendor. Aisle 31 in the Proverbs section had clothes made of strength and dignity on rack 25. "Laughing with no fear of the future" was the finishing touch to this outfit.

In the Psalm section, isle 30 on rack 5, I found clothes of joy. As I walked through different sections, I saw complete ensembles beautifully displayed. The attendant told me the Designer created these ensembles to take the guesswork out of trying to make each piece coordinate well to create a complete look.

In the Colossians section on aisle 3, I found an ensemble for those who are "God's chosen people, holy and dearly loved" on rack 12. It was made with compassion, kindness, humility, gentleness and patience.

The ensemble on rack 27, aisle 3 in Galatians was for "those who were baptized into Christ" and "clothed with Christ." I also found the same ensemble in aisle 3, rack 18 in The Revelation section.

Fashion Tip #16
To pull together an overall look, current fashion trends suggest putting on clothing of righteousness and justice as your robe and turban

Job 29:14

Seasonal dressing is key, so I looked for fashions designed for seasons:

- When your soul rejoices in God, wear garments of salvation, arrayed in a robe of righteousness (Isaiah 61:10).

- In times when you do not think about how to gratify the

desires of the sinful nature, clothe yourself with the Lord Jesus Christ (Romans 13:14).

- When we are self-controlled, put on the armor of faith and love and the hope of salvation as our helmet (1 Thessalonians 5:8).

As I made my way through the boutique, I just couldn't pass up the accessories I saw in Ephesians. I found all of these exclusive accessories down aisle 6 on tables 14 through 17.

- The Hat; the helmet of salvation (Ephesians 6:17).

- The Belt; "Stand firm then, with the belt of truth buckled around your waist" (Ephesians 6:14).

- The Vest; the breastplate of righteousness (Ephesians 6:14).

- The Jacket; the shield of faith, with which you can extinguish all the flaming arrows of the evil one (Ephesians 6:16).

- The Shoes; your feet fitted with the readiness that comes from the gospel of peace (Ephesians 6:15).

- The Purse; the sword of the Spirit, which is the word of God (Ephesians 6:17).

As I made my way through the boutique, I gathered up my things and went over to the checkout to pay for them. The cashier told me to put my money away. She said I owed nothing. She said the Designer paid the price for me in full! I knew I was in a special place when I received so much and paid nothing!

After I finished at the checkout, I felt I had to meet the Designer. I wanted to personally thank Him for all He'd given to me. I wanted to get His autograph, but I didn't have anything for Him to write on, so I decided I wanted Him to write His name on my heart, and when He did I was thrilled. My life was changed forever.

Just as I was about to leave, the attendant at the desk called me over. She told me she couldn't let me leave without first giving me a free gift. I love gifts, so I gladly walked over to her. She handed me a package. I noticed it had my name on it and was signed by the Designer himself. So I quickly tore off the covering and inside I received my free gift—salvation!

I'm sure you can tell from my personal shopping experience why I am so excited to share the Good News with you. My hope is that you'll take time to look for and find this exclusive boutique for yourself. Isn't it worth it to have the privilege of having your name written in the book, to receive so much, and have it all prepaid for you? It will be worth the time and effort you put into looking for it!

When you find it for yourself, get excited and share the Good News with all those you love and care for. Here we are! Watch your step as you detrain.

Oh by the way, your fashion designer is God. His designer label is *King of Kings and* LORD *of* LORDS. On the part of the robe that covered his thigh was written, 'King of Kings and LORD of LORDS'"(Revelation 19:16, TLB), and the name of this exclusive boutique? *The Bible.*

If after shopping in the Bible you don't find your passion for this fashion, feel free to come back and visit again. It's open twenty-four hours, seven days a week. The Light will always be on and your fashion designer will always be there waiting to welcome you!

The Look

Okay…you're in the dressing room trying on some fashions. You admire your self in the mirror and think *Umm…not bad.* You turn around to face your friend and say,

"How do I look?"

When you ask the question, are you prepared for the answer? When it comes to fashion, it's "the Look" that counts. When I pick up something I think is cute and my sister disagrees, she says, "Lisa, put that down and step away from the ugly outfit!" How we think determines how we see things and how we see things determines how we look. The mind doesn't have eyes but it can see beyond imagination.

Have you heard the expression "the eyes are the windows to the soul"? Seeing things from the inside out gives perspective. Perspective is funny thing; it changes depending on your vantage point. Do you look down on the things you don't have or do you see the blessings in all you do have?

"Keep your eyes focused on what is right and look straight ahead to what is good" (Proverbs 4:25, NCV).

When Jesus looked at the prostitute and told her, her sins were forgiven, how do you think she looked? Can you imagine how Adam and Eve looked the first time they saw they were naked? What did Moses look like when he came down from the mountain with the Ten Commandments in his arms? The look of God shown on his face. Did little David look up at Goliath and see victory?

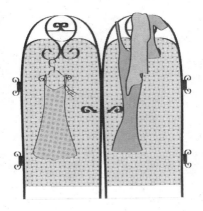

God's fashions look good on us when we see the purpose for wearing them. In the dressing room is where we see ourselves. When you put on faith, do you see God in it? Does his joy look hopeful when you see it on you? Does trying on patience make you see the strength in it? It's all about the Look.

In the story of Snow White, the queen looked into the magic mirror and asked the question "Mirror, mirror on the wall, who's the fairest of them all?" She let the mirror decide how she looked and as long as the mirror answered, "You are," she was content. But the moment the mirror decided she was no longer "the fairest one of all," she freaked! She felt that way because she let the mirror determine her perspective.

"My dear friends, don't let public opinion influence how you live out our glorious, Christ-oriented faith" (James 2:1, MSG).

Perspective gives us the option to choose how we look. Looking through our own sinful eyes we may see no hope, but seeing through the eyes of God looks hopeful.

If you're not sure how you look, here's some "fashion looks" for you to see:

"But if we look forward to some things we don't have yet, we must wait patiently and confidently"

Romans 8:25, NLT

"We have seen and testify that the Father has sent the Son and Savior of the world"

1 John 4:14, NASB

"Keep your eyes focused on what is right and look straight ahead to what is good"

Proverbs 4:25, NCV

"Let us fix our eyes on Jesus, the author and perfecter of our faith, who for the joy set before him endured the cross, scorning its shame and sat down at the right hand of the throne of God"

Hebrews 12:2

Seeing is believing! G*S.T.Y.L.E.!

Conclusion

When I was little, I loved to go to my Grandmother Ina's house. She saved the Sunday papers for me and my sister to get the paper dolls from. We'd spend hours cutting out all of the beautiful clothes to put on them.

My grandmother had a wooden chest she kept at the foot of her bed filled with "dress up" clothes and accessories for us to put on and play with. My mom and my grandmother enjoyed watching us as we played and laughed and modeled our clothes for them.

I believe God smiles every time He sees us truly enjoying the fashions He has for us. He gives us life to be enjoyed, to find pleasure in the abundance He provides. Those clothes my grandmother saved up and handed down were given in love simply for us to enjoy. The Father saves up and hands down His very best to us, in unconditional love for us to enjoy.

"How great is the love the Father has lavished on us, that we should be called children of God! And that is what we are!" (1 John 3:1).

I will always remember those days spent at my grandmother's house because they hold such fun and joyful memories.

Be Fashion conscience. Use the good fashion sense that God gives you. Read your Fashion Guide often. Wear must-have and stand-out fashions that bring glory to God, and always accessorize with His mercy and saving grace to make your outfit complete. Pass on your passion for the LORD to others. Confidently walk down the runway of life with your head held high knowing you are modeling what God intended you to wear.

I hope and pray you have enjoyed reading this book as much as I have enjoyed writing it for you. I passionately look forward to seeing you wear God's fashions in G*S.T.Y.L.E.!

Fashion Extras

The Fashion Guide

Have you ever looked at the Bible as a fashion guide? Did you know the Bible contains past and present fashions, advice on fashion sense, fashion trends and a bio on the creator of fashion?

I know you're probably saying to yourself, "Lisa, that's crazy! The Bible is a history book. The Bible has nothing to do with fashion let alone giving me fashion advise." Would you be willing to believe me if I prove to you that God's fashion is full of passion? After all, are we not uniquely "fashioned" (made in His image) by God Himself?

So, did I peak your curiosity? Would you be willing to at least see if I'm right?

Those with a mature understanding of the Bible see it as more than just a history book or a book of prophesies written by people who lived long ago. We who are developing our passion for God need to understand the Bible is God-breathed not man-made. It's important to know that fact because the wisdom and truth of the Bible never changes. It *was, is* and *always will be.* There's no other book on earth that can make that claim.

Some people avoid reading the Bible thinking it's too hard to understand. What they fail to realize is the key to understanding is in the approach. Everyone knows that most vehicles have a blind spot. Even though we have a rear view mirror and two side mirrors, we can miss seeing the car right beside us. It's not until we turn to look that we discover a car is there. If we accept that blind spots exist, our approach will always be to look first before we turn into the next lane.

When we approach the Bible with the understanding that there will be blind spots, we can always turn and look to God in prayer to reveal His truth before we turn the page.

Some contemporary thinkers believe we should only read the Bible when we have been "good enough" because it's God's Holy Word. There are many writers of Scripture who didn't feel worthy to write God's Word, but he approved them and directed their hearts. Even when we don't feel worthy or feel we fall too short, God approves us to read the Bible.

If we take the viewpoint that the Bible is God's guide for daily living, it may seem less intimidating to read. I call it our

Fashion Guide to fall in line with the theme of this book, and to present it as our guide for fashion trends, fashion advice, fashion sense, and to give insight to wearing God's fashions. Our Fashion Guide references people who've worn His fashions and leads us to know the Designer. He fashioned (equipped) us on purpose, and wants us to read our Fashion Guide regularly and with passion.

What to Wear to the Wedding

The twenty-four elders and the four living creatures fell down and worshiped God, who was seated on the throne. And they cried, "Amen, Hallelujah!"

> Then a voice came from the throne, saying: "Praise our God, all you his servants, you who fear him, both small and great!" Then I heard what sounded like a great multitude, like the roar of rushing waters and like loud pearls of thunder, shouting: "Hallelujah! For our LORD God Almighty reigns. Let us rejoice and be glad and give him glory! For the wedding of the Lamb has come, and his bride has made herself ready. Fine linen, bright and clean, was given her to wear." (Fine linen stands for the righteous acts of the saints.) Then the angel said to me, "Write: 'Blessed are those who are invited to the wedding supper of the Lamb!' " And he added, "These are the true words of God."
>
> At this I fell at his feet to worship him. But he said to me, "Do not do it! I am a fellow servant with you and with your brothers who hold to the testimony of Jesus. Worship God! For the testimony of Jesus is the spirit of prophecy."
>
> Revelation 19:4–10

Kingdom Dressing—
Dress for Success

The fashion conscience "dress to impress," but heirs to the Kingdom "dress for success." Kingdom heirs (that's you!) are supernaturally dressed for successful living.

I view dressing as spiritual gifts. This is different from being clothed in Christ. Spiritual gifts are God-given for us to use. Being clothed in Christ means we have His spirit within us. I believe we are successful when we use the gifts God gives us to bring glory to Him. He gives us the tools ("give us this day our daily bread") to carry out His will for us.

Paul was *formally* dressed for success in preaching just as pastors are today. God equips them with inspiration and the voice to preach the Word with formal training. Peter was *supernaturally* dressed for healing when the tongues of fire were placed on him at Pentecost. Solomon was *wisely* dressed to succeed as a king. David was dressed in *courage* to succeed in victory against Goliath. God gives us wisdom and courage to defeat the giants we face in life.

Givers are *abundantly* dressed to successfully give with the right heart. Believers are supernaturally dressed for successful living. Here are some successfully dressed examples found in our Fashion Guide, along with some success tips to keep you successfully dressed for the Kingdom!

> "That's what will make you successful, following the directions and doing the things that God commanded Moses for Israel. Courage! Take charge! Don't be timid; don't hold back"
>
> 1 Chronicles 22:13, MSG

"Everything he took up, whether it had to do with worship in God's Temple or the carrying out of God's Law and Commandments, he did well in a spirit of prayerful worship. He was a great success"

2 Chronicles 31:21, MSG

"John answered, "It's not possible for a person to succeed—I'm talking about eternal success—without heaven's help"

John 3:27, MSG

"Be strong and very courageous. Be careful to obey all the law my servant Moses gave you; do not turn from it to the right or to the left, that you may be successful wherever you go"

Joshua 1:7

"Do not let this Book of the Law depart from your mouth; meditate on it day and night, so that you may be careful to do everything written in it. Then you will be prosperous and successful"

Joshua 1:8

"O LORD, save us; O LORD, grant us success"

Psalm 118:25

"If the ax is dull and its edge unsharpened, more strength is needed but skill will bring success"

Ecclesiastes 10:10

Dry Cleaning

Some fashions require dry cleaning. They need special treatment to get dirt out and be refreshed. "Repent, then, and turn to God, so that your sins may be wiped out, that times of refreshing may come from the Lord, and that he may send the Christ, who has been appointed for you—even Jesus" (Acts 3:19–21).

Baptism washes us into new life. We need only be baptized once, but we should repent often (dry cleaning).

"Peter replied, "Repent and be baptized, every one of you, in the name of Jesus Christ for the forgiveness of your sins. And you will receive the gift of the Holy Spirit"

Acts 2:38

"The Lord is not slow in keeping his promise, as some understand slowness. He is patient with you, not wanting anyone to perish, but everyone to come to repentance"

2 Peter 3:9

"In the same way, I tell you, there is rejoicing in the presence of the angels of God over one sinner who repents"

Luke 15:10

"I baptize you with water for repentance. But after me will come one who is more powerful than I, whose sandals I am not fit to carry. He will baptize you with the Holy Spirit and with fire"

Matthew 3:11

Parking

You may think that parking doesn't have anything to do with developing a passion for God's fashion. But let's look around the parking lot to see if we can find a connection!

I think finding a parking space is like prayer. When we go shopping we usually have to drive there first, find a parking spot and walk to the mall. Parking lots have solid white lines that define the space we park in much like God's will. When we pray, our prayers are answered according to His will (within the lines). "This is the confidence we have in approaching God: that if we ask anything according to his will, he hears us" (1 John 5:14).

God knows the desires of our heart before we ask Him and we must trust that when we seek Him in prayer, he will answer according to what is best for us. "And if we know that he hears us—whatever we ask—we know that we have what we asked of him" (1 John 5:15).

In Northern Virginia, we have one of the largest outlet malls on the east coast (Potomac Mills), and during certain times of the year it's really hard to find a parking space. There are usually plenty of parking spaces, but when so many people come to shop from different parts of the country, spaces (especially up front) can be hard to find. Sometimes we may feel distant from God. We pray for answers and circle the parking lot many times. When we are forced to park farther away, it doesn't mean that God hasn't answered our prayer. We just have to walk a little farther to get to where we want to be. Walking is exercise. The disciples asked Jesus to teach them how to pray.

One day Jesus was praying in a certain place. When he finished, one of his disciples said to him, "LORD, teach us to pray, just as John taught his disciples." He said to them,

"When you pray, say: 'Father, hallowed be your name, your
kingdom come. Give us each day our daily bread. Forgive
us our sins, for we also forgive everyone who sins against us.
And lead us not into temptation.'"

Luke 11:1–4

By exercising prayer, we discover how God answers them.
We may pray to acquire some thing and God may answer by
giving us the knowledge to acquire it. It may seem as though
it hasn't been answered (because we don't see the physical evi-
dence), but the answer may be right in front of us (in God's time
not ours), like when a car pulls out of a parking space at the same
time we approach the area.

"Ask and it will be given to you; seek and you will find;
knock and the door will be opened to you. For everyone
who asks receives; he who seeks finds; and to him who
knocks, the door will be opened"

Matthew 7:7–8

Sometimes it may appear a space is open, but as we make our
way around the parking lot, we discover a motorcycle occupying
the space! That lets us know we need to look in another direction
than we first thought to find the answer. We can know prayers
are being answered when God works things out to line up with
his will for us.

I drive an SUV and sometimes I have to back up first to
straighten out in order to pull into the space. When you think
God is pointing you in a certain direction, look back at your circumstances, wisdom in our Fashion Guide, and wise words from
those you trust to validate (line up with) what you're thinking is
correct. Then you can pull into the parking space.

Some parking lots have valet services that allow us to park in front and let someone else park our car while we shop. When we are in the will of God (knowing His direction for us), we can pull up in front and walk a short distance to shop for his fashions!

I think now you see the connection. Go to God in prayer. Ask, seek, find, knock and receive!

> "So I say to you: Ask and it will be given to you; seek and you will find; knock and the door will be opened to you. For everyone who asks receives; he who seeks finds; and to him who knocks, the door will be opened"
>
> Luke 11:9–10